HORRIBLE SCIENCE

THE AWFULLY BIG QUIZ BOOK

NICK ARNOLD
TONY DE SAULLES

■ SCHOLASTIC

Scholastic Children's Books,
Commonwealth House, 1-19 New Oxford Street
London WC1A 1NU, UK

A division of Scholastic Ltd
London ~ New York ~ Toronto ~ Sydney ~ Auckland
Mexico City ~ New Delhi ~ Hong Kong

First published in the UK by Scholastic Ltd, 2000

ISBN 0 439 99750 X

Typeset by Falcon Oast Graphic Art, East Hoathly, Sussex
Printed by WS Bookwell, Finland

10 9 8 7 6 5 4 3 2 1

Contents

Introduction

Science is full of facts and teachers seem to know them all…

So wouldn't it be FANTABULOUS if there was a book with HUNDREDS of facts your teacher *didn't* know! This could totally transform your life...

And just imagine if this book was packed with quizzes and cartoons and even had special impossible questions for teachers! Now that would *really* liven up your Science lessons...

And if that isn't enough, just imagine if this book was overflowing with horrible facts – the sort of facts that make Science really *horrible*. (Horrible *fun* that is.)

Well, you don't have to imagine any more because at this *very* second you're holding the *very book* we've been talking about! So stop dreaming and get reading!

Murderous medicine

Medicine is a life or death science. That's to say, medicine aims to cure or prevent disease and study the human body. It's an awfully big "body" of knowledge, but let's find a medical scientist to explain what they do...

HORRIBLE SCIENCE PROFILES 1

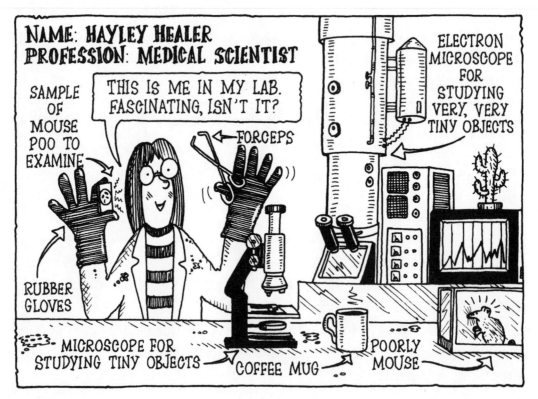

We medical scientists study how disease affects the body and how the body fights back. Some of us work in universities and some of us work for drug companies. Me, I'm at university looking at how the guts defend themselves against tiny germs called viruses. Right now I'm looking at mice with the viruses in their guts, but later on I'll be looking at humans and I'll need some human volunteers to study – anyone want to sign up for testing?

And talking about testing – are you ready for the first medical quiz?

YOU CAN COUNT UP YOUR SCORE AND CHECK ON YOUR PROGRESS ON THE SCOREBOARD AT THE END OF EACH CHAPTER.

Have a go body quiz

EACH QUESTION HAS ONLY TWO POSSIBLE ANSWERS – SO EVEN IF YOU JUST GUESS YOU'VE STILL GOT A 50 PER CENT CHANCE OF BEING RIGHT!

1 Who has the highest body temperature? Boys or ~~girls~~? ✗
2 What can human teenagers do that chimps can't do? ~~Change a light bulb~~/have a growth spurt during their adolescence. ✓
3 What can a canary do that your mum or dad can't do? ~~Sing~~/re-shape their brain. ✓
4 On a dark night your eyes can spot a match being struck how far away? ~~80.5 km (50 miles)~~/100 metres (328 feet). ✗

5 What can a human do that a budgie can't do? ~~Play a tune by farting~~/blink. ✗

Answers (total score five points):

1 Girls, by 0.3°C. And no, boys, that doesn't make you "cooler" than girls.

2 Chimps *can* be trained to change light bulbs, but humans are the only animals that grow faster as they change from youngsters into adults.

3 Canaries increase their brain size each Spring when they learn new songs. I expect they feel right tweets if they get the songs wrong!

4 80.5 km – it's true!

5 Play a tune with their bottom! Several performers could do this – the most famous, Frenchman Joseph Pujol (1857-1945), could also play the flute and blow out candles with his musical rear end. It's said that when he lay dying he performed the last post.

THAT WAS MOVING ... EXTREMELY SMELLY BUT MOVING

HORRIBLE HEALTH WARNING!

Can you do this? If so, do NOT demonstrate this interesting skill at family mealtimes. Otherwise, you could find yourself sharing your meal with the dog.

Could you be a doctor?

1 In 1905 Frenchman Dr Beurieux examined the newly-chopped-off head of a murderer. What did he discover?

a) The lips murmured "I must have laughed my head off!"

b) The head opened its eyes each time its name was called. √

c) The head did nothing – it was a dead head.

Answer (one point):
b) The brain can survive without its blood supply from the body for a few minutes. But talking about the eyes...

Dare you discover ... how your eyeballs roll?

FOR **DARE YOU DISCOVER** QUESTIONS ALL YOU HAVE TO DO IS TRY THE EXPERIMENT AND YOU'LL GET THE ANSWER. THE GOOD NEWS IS THAT YOU COULD WIN A WHOLE FOUR POINTS!

What you need:
One set of eyeballs. (You might need a spare set if you lose the first one.)

What you do:
Read and memorize these instructions. Alternatively, you could write them on the inside of your eyelids or ask a friend to read them to you.
• Close your eyes.
• Imagine you're looking at something high up and roll your eyeballs upwards. Keep your head level.
• Try to open your eyes.

What do you notice?

Answer (four points):
You can't open your eyes – so DON'T force them! Just roll your eyeballs back down and you can open your eyelids normally. The muscles that open your eyes also roll your eyeballs up but they can't do two things at once. By the way, if a monster rolls its eyeballs at you – it's only polite to pick them up and roll them back.

Add 'em up quiz

All you need to do in this quiz is calculate the answers – it's that simple. And you can even use a calculator if you want! Now, is that easy or what?

To begin with add 26 to 34.

1 How many bones are babies born with? (Multiply your last answer ✗ by five.)

2 How many muscles do you have? (Add 350.) ✗

NOT MANY!

PIMPLE, ER, I MEAN MUSCLE

3 How many joints do you have? (Add 50 and divide by seven.) ✗

4 How many kilometres of blood vessels do you have? (Multiply by ✗ 1,000.)

5 How many times can your nerves stretch round the world? (Minus ✗ 99,996.25.)

6 If you used all the power produced by your muscles in one day how far in metres could you lift your dad's car into the air? (Add 1.25 and multiply by three.) ✗

7 How many red blood cells does your body make in a minute? (Just ✗ in case you didn't know – cells are the tiny jelly-like living objects that make up your body.) (Multiply by 100,000 and take away 300,000.)

8 How many hairs do you lose a day? (Take away 200,000 and divide ✗ by 10,000.)

HEE HEE! THEY'LL NEVER GUESS THIS ONE

9 How many germs live in each square millimetre of your armpits? (The posh word for germs is bacteria.) (Multiply by eight.) ✗

10 How long in millimetres is the smallest muscle in your body? (Divide by 800.) ✗

Foul feeding

Feeding is one of the most fascinating activities the body does. Here's a quiz involving facts that even hard-boiled doctors would find hard to stomach...

Rotten recipes quiz

Some humans will happily eat anything, even (it's been rumoured) *school dinners*. Which TWO items on this menu have NEVER been eaten by humans?

11

3) **Human body soup.** (A 160-year-old corpse cooked inside a lead coffin in a fire to make a nutritious soup.)

MAIN COURSES:

4) **Crispy dinosaur eyeballs.**

5) **65-year-old beef.**

6) **Cigarettes on pizza.**

7) **Toasted dung beetle.** (Delicious eggy soufflé taste with a crispy outside.) Served with boiled cod and snail sauce. All main dishes are served with

(8) a **bowl of cement,** and

(9) a **birch twig side salad.**

DESSERT MENU

10) **Spamalamadingdong.** (A delicious slice of canned pork in a meaty jelly covered in chocolate and whipped cream.)

11) **Giant tubeworm sundae.** (Deep sea worm filled with a slimy bacteria, with butterscotch sauce.)

After your meal:

12) Use a **toothbrush** (then eat it).

Answers (one point each):

4 No one has ever found a dinosaur eyeball because they rotted away before they could become fossils.

11 The giant tubeworms were only discovered in the 1970s and as far as I know no scientist has ever dared eat one – but, if you're volunteering...

Foul food facts

Here are some disgusting facts your teacher won't know about the other foods. It's OK – this isn't a quiz so you can relax for a few minutes...

1 Two visitors to an Essex church tried this delicacy in 1779. They reported that it tasted of olives.

2 The Wallishauser family of Germany ate their granny's ashes by accident in the 1940s. The ashes had been sent from the USA by relatives and the family thought they were some kind of American soup mix.

3 John Colet was buried in a lead coffin. When St. Paul's Cathedral was burnt down in 1666 two men drank the disgusting goo that was all that remained of John Colet.

5 A British Navy speciality – in the 1870s they were still eating beef salted in 1805.

6 This recipe was invented by a man named Wes Haskins of Nevada, USA. He eats raw cigarettes too. (*Don't* try this at home.)

7 This recipe was invented by insect food fanatic W.S. Bristowe in the 1920s – I expect it was his favourite grub. Cod and snail sauce was a favourite of Victorian insect eater Vincent Holt.

8 Yes, a bag of cement was eaten by another American John W. Horton, but he sicked it up again. (*Definitely* don't try this at home.)

9 Yet another American Jay Gwaltrey ate a birch tree. It took him 89 hours – wood you believe it? (You're not wooden-headed enough to try this, so I don't have to warn you ... do I?)

10 The meat was called Spam and this delicacy was eaten at the 1994 Spamarama Festival in Texas. A visitor named Bob Finlay ate it and commented:

12 Japanese Otoichi Kawakami ate 56 toothbrushes and various other objects as a bet. Anyone silly enough to eat toothbrushes deserves a good pasting.

Bonus question

For a bonus question you get not one but **TWO** points – that's why it's called a BONUS question!

Why is it dangerous for surgeons to operate on the guts using electrically heated instruments? (Clue: BANG!) ✓✓

Answer (two points):
Fart gas can contain methane, an explosive substance also found in cooking gas. There have been cases of the gas in patients' guts exploding with messy results. One man was seen with blue flames coming out of his backside (and I expect the surgeon responsible was fired).

Well, that's enough dangerous patients – now for some facts about dangerous *doctors*...

Dangerous doctors
For most of history doctors were so ignorant of disease they were a menace. If you were at death's door and you saw the doc he'd probably push you through...

Could you be a doctor?
1 It's 200 years ago and you're using leeches to suck a patient's blood. (In those days disease was supposed to be caused by having too much blood.) The leeches are full up – what do you do? (Clue: Teach them a sharp lesson.)

a) Make them sick up the blood and start feeding again. ✓

b) Look for a vampire bat.

c) Cut off the leeches' tails so that the patient's blood squirts out from the wound.

2 Although arteries are blood vessels the word actually means "air carrier". Why? (Clue: Blood? I see no blood!)

a) Arteries can be used to make wind instruments.

b) Someone muddled an artery up with the windpipe.

c) The ancient Greeks thought that arteries carried air. ✓

3 Indian surgeon Susrata (who lived about AD 450) developed the first operation for cataracts (cloudy areas on the outer part of the eyeball). What did he practise on? (Clue: It's crunch time!)

a) Toads

b) His own eyeballs

c) Pickled onions ✓

Answers (total score three points):

1 c) The leeches will carry on feeding!

2 c) Ancient Greek doctor Praxagoras (Fourth Century BC) cut up a dead body and found the arteries empty and drained of blood.

3 c) Pickled onions. He practised next on a bag of slime and the operation proved to be successful.

Disgusting diseases

When the body gets sick it might suffer from a fascinating array of disgusting diseases. This section has all the foul facts you need...

Strange sick note quiz

Over the page is a selection of sick notes. Which ones describe *genuine* medical problems and which don't? (Clue: TWO of the notes have been forged!)

1

Dear Teacher,

My daughter Chloe has geophagy.* This is a medical condition in which the sufferer feels an over-whelming urge to eat earth. Please excuse her from cookery lessons because she might want to make a mud pie for my supper.

(* Note, that's not *geography*. Geography isn't actually an illness – although it can be a pain in the neck.)

2

Dear Teacher,

My son Jack has vasomotor rhinitis (va-so-mo-tor ri-ni-tis). His nose runs when he goes into a cold place. I think it must be something he's inherited because Jack's nose runs in the family.

3

Dear Teacher,

My son Stephen has auto-intoxication (or-to in-tox-ick-cay-shun). Rotting poo from his guts has got into his blood. This awful disease causes baldness and bad breath – and it's made him too ugly to go to school. Please excuse him from lessons for the next 23 years.

4

Dear Teacher,

My daughter Amy has a glimmering gizzard. It's got so bad her liver actually glows in the dark! And to think – she used to be a shining example of good health.

5

Dear Teacher,
My son Michael has a lung disease called
Pneumonoultramicroscopicsilicovolcanoconiosis.* Coughing his
little lungs out he is. Please give him a breathing space
from lessons.

* That's new-mo-nool-tra-mi-cro-scop-pic-sill-lick-co-vol-cay-no-co-nee-o-sis.

6

Mon cher Teacher,
Ah apologize foor my poor daughter Rachel — she suffers
from ze Foreign Aczent Syndrom. Zoot alors! Mais oui, she
onlee talk in ze French aczent! Pleeze excuse 'er from allez
ze lessons (except La Francais, of course!).

Answers (total score six points):

1 TRUE. Some clays mix with poisons in the stomach and stop you from getting poisoned. But soil is full of germs so don't try eating your garden.

2 TRUE. Do you get it?

3 FALSE. But the Victorians believed there was such a disease and that it was caused by constipation.

4 FALSE. This disease was featured in a 1677 medical advert. The authors couldn't think of enough real diseases so they made a few up!

5 TRUE. It's a lung disease caused by breathing in tiny bits of ash from volcanoes.

6 TRUE. It's a rare disease in which the sufferer can only speak in a foreign accent — honestly! In 1999 a British woman developed the condition after a brain seizure. She could only speak in a French accent despite the fact that she had only been to France once and didn't speak the language.

Bonus point

You can have an extra two points if you can say **Pneumonoultramicroscopicsilicovolcanoconiosis** quickly and correctly *four* times. You can have as many tries as you like but you need a witness to check that you got it right. (Clue: Try breaking the word up into three parts and practising each part before putting them together.)

Answer (two points):
Well, did you manage it? Now casually drop it into a Science lesson and gobsmack the entire class!

Odd cure out quiz

ONE of these substances has NEVER been used as a medical treatment. There's one point for getting the substance and another point for explaining why it's never been used.

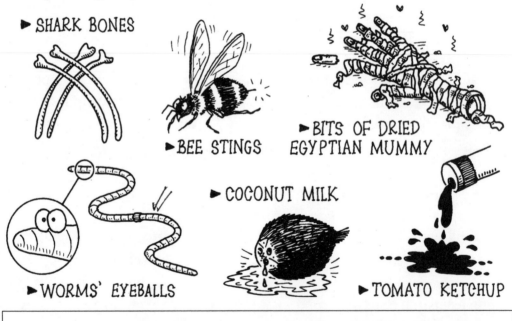

► SHARK BONES

►BEE STINGS

►BITS OF DRIED EGYPTIAN MUMMY

► COCONUT MILK

►WORMS' EYEBALLS

►TOMATO KETCHUP

Answer (two points):
Worms' eyeballs. And the reason this has never been used as a treatment is because worms don't actually have eyeballs – they have patches of sensitive skin that detect light. And now for some facts that your teacher won't know about the other cures...

• Artificial skin was developed by US scientist Ioannis Yannis in 1981. It contains a chemical made from shark bones.

• Bee stings were a traditional cure for rheumatism.

• Ancient Egyptian body parts were shipped to Europe in the Middle Ages for use as medicine. French King Francis I (1494-1547) used to munch on a lump of preserved human flesh every time he felt unwell. Oh well, you can't beat mummy's cooking.

• During the Second World War, coconut milk was used as a substitute for plasma (the watery stuff in the blood) on the island of Fiji and worked very well.

• In the 1830s tomato sauce was on sale in the USA as a medicine that could cure just about anything.

So how did you get on?

Congratulations on finishing this chapter! Have you got new facts coming out of your ears?

Here's what your score means...

OK, now you've pulled yourself together are you ready to push on? Talking about pushing and pulling, they're both forces and forces **are** part of an AWFULLY BIG branch of Science ... as you're about to discover...

FEARSOME BIT HAPPENS HERE!

Fearsome physics

This chapter is packed with quizzes and horrible facts about physics – the branch of science that deals with atoms and forces. It sounds awfully technical and awfully baffling – but fortunately we've found a physicist to explain what she's up to...

HORRIBLE SCIENCE PROFILES 2

NAME: SALLY STAYBRIGHT
PROFESSION: PHYSICIST

HERE I AM IN MY LAB, SORRY ABOUT THE MESS

ELECTROMAGNET (A MAGNET WHICH IS POWERED BY AN ELECTRIC CURRENT)

COMPUTER TO CONTROL MASER (A MACHINE FOR MAKING MICROWAVES)

SOUP

COMPUTER (FOR SHOWING GRAPHICS OF THE MOVEMENTS OF ATOMS)

MICROWAVE OVEN (A MACHINE FOR HEATING UP SOUP)

NOTEBOOK

*B*eing a physicist, I'm interested in forces and energy and atoms and topics such as light and electricity and sound and how things move. (Not *too* much to get to grips with, then!) We physicists usually work in teams because each project involves loads of work and it helps to share out the duties. That's why I'm here at university working as part of a team investigating how magnetism affects microwaves. (Microwaves are the invisible waves of energy made inside a microwave oven.) The work involves setting up loads of experiments – this really is a testing job!

All physicists have one thing in common – they've all studied the work of superstar physicist Isaac Newton (1642-1727). Isaac Newton showed by experiment that sunlight is made up of all colours of light mixed together, and he explained how all the forces in the universe operate, including gravity. Just think – he managed to explain the science of how planes and rockets flew before they were even invented!

Well, here are some obscure facts about this scientific genius that 99 per cent of physicists won't know...

Could you think like Newton?
1 YOU are Isaac Newton. You're doing your Science homework but the cat keeps wanting to come in and then go out again. What do you do?
a) Lock her in the shed.
b) Invent the cat flap. √

2 Your neighbour spots you foaming at the mouth one day. In fact, you're blowing bubbles – but why?

a) You're playing with the cat.

b) You're studying the way the bubbles bend light.

3 After you become a famous scientist, some people think you have ✓ magical powers and a woman asks you to use magic to find her lost purse. What do you say?

a)

GET LOST, YOU SILLY OLD CRONE!

b) You say the magic word "ABRACADABRA" and send her off to ✓ look around the Royal Naval Hospital in Greenwich.

4 You fall out with your fellow scientist Robert Hooke after he claims your experiments on light don't work properly. What do you do?

a) Delay publishing your work on light until Hooke is dead so he can't ✓ have a go at you.

R·I·P R.HOOKE 1635~1703

IT'S A GRAVE SITUATION ...YIPPEE!

b) Publish the work immediately and ask Hooke to make constructive comments.

5 You reckon your theory of gravity can predict the effects of gravity on an object to an accuracy of 0.00003 per cent. How do you persuade other scientists of this?

a) You spend years trying to prove the accuracy of your prediction. ✗

b) You ask your publisher to print a fiddled set of figures that appear to show this result.

6 You take charge of Britain's coinage. Part of the job involves tracking down people who make fake coins, and by bribing informers and listening to gossip in shady pubs you eventually trap master forger William Chaloner. The penalty for forgery is death and the criminal begs for mercy. What do you do?

a) You arrange to have him executed in an especially cruel and disgusting fashion.

ARGH, THAT'S FREEZING!

ERK, THAT'S BOILING!

CENSORED!

OUCH, THAT'S SHARP!

N-N-NO THAT'S **ARGH!**

b) You ask the king to spare William's life. ✗

Answers (total score six points):

1 b) Newton actually invented the cat flap! He built the first one at the farmhouse where he grew up. When the cat had kittens he made a mini cat flap for them to use.

2 b) The sides of the bubble bend light until it breaks into the colours that make it up. That's why you can see rainbows in bubbles.

3 b) Newton just wanted to get rid of the woman but according to the story that's where the purse was found!

4 a)

5 b) It's shocking ... but true!

6 a) Newton had William Chaloner hanged until he was half-dead and then cut down to have his guts pulled out and his body chopped into pieces and his head cut off. (I expect he was 100 per cent dead after that.)

Bonus question

Newton's dog, Diamond, knocked over a candle and caused a fire that destroyed years of Newton's work on light. What did the scientist say?

a) SAY YOUR PRAYERS, MUTT – YOU'RE HISTORY!

b) THAT'S ALRIGHT OLD BOY – ACCIDENTS HAPPEN!

c) O DIAMOND, DIAMOND, YOU LITTLE KNOW THE DAMAGE YOU HAVE DONE! ✓

Frightening forces quiz

Forces affect the movement of an object – but which of these are forces facts and which are forces fiction? Answer TRUE or FALSE.

1 Long train tunnels are built in pairs and linked by cross passages to allow air to escape from the tunnel.

2 New Kansai International airport in Japan is designed to sink.

3 Water can be used to cut metal, rock, leather and paper.

4 The force of gravity makes you taller.

5 In a storm, a loaded supertanker bends in the middle by up to 90 cm (3 feet).

6 Weight is one measure of the gravity acting on an object. The air weighs more than the sea.

7 The force of the wind is enough to slow the spin of planet Earth.

8 Good weather makes you thinner.

9 Scientists have found that jumping around like a kangaroo requires less energy than running.

10 If you run west you'll weigh less than if you run east.

11 In the 1840s a ship from Uruguay, South America, fired balls of cheese to beat off an attacking ship.

Answers (total score eleven points):

1 TRUE. When a train goes though a long tunnel it pushes air in front of it. In a large tunnel this can slow the train. The cross passages prevent this problem by allowing the air to escape.

2 TRUE. The airport is built on an artificial island and it's expected to sink under the weight of the buildings by 11-13 metres (12-14 feet) in 30 years.

3 TRUE. In industry, water-cutting uses fine high-pressure sprays mixed with tiny bits of grit.

4 FALSE. Gravity makes you *shorter!* Every night you grow around 8 mm (0.3 inches) because when you lie down gravity isn't pushing down on your spine. This means that you wake up taller in the morning and shrink during the day!

5 TRUE. If it bent any more it would snap.

6 FALSE. The air weighs 50,000,000,000,000,000 (50 million billion) tonnes, give or take a few grams, but that's only one-third the weight of the sea.

7 TRUE. But not so as you'd notice, otherwise windy days would last for ever as the Earth stopped turning in space.

8 TRUE. In bright sunny weather the air pressure is greater and this squeezes your bulging body and makes you feel leaner and fitter. In miserable overcast weather the opposite happens and your body feels bloated and squashy.

9 TRUE. In the 1970s two scientists monitored how much oxygen kangaroos needed to breathe and found they needed less than running humans.

10 FALSE. It's the opposite way round! As you travel east the spin of the Earth pulls on your body and slightly reduces your weight. This effect is also too small to notice.

11 TRUE. The faster something moves the harder it hits you. Fired like cannon balls the hard Edam cheeses were moving fast enough to kill several sailors and wreck the sails of the attacking ship, forcing it to retreat. Hard cheese to them, then.

Bonus question

Why do ships have round portholes? (Clue: That's torn it!)

Answer (two points):
The force of the waves sends shock waves through a metal ship and the buckling effect could tear the corners of square portholes. Wooden ships can have square windows because wood is better at soaking up the shock waves.

Awful accidents quiz

In this quiz you have to say what happened next...

OK, IT'S HARD TO GET THESE EXACTLY RIGHT – SO I TELL YOU WHAT, YOU CAN HAVE ONE POINT FOR EACH ROUGHLY CORRECT ANSWER AND TWO POINTS FOR GETTING AN ANSWER EXACTLY RIGHT!

1 December 1916 – the Alpine mountains were covered in deep snow. One Austrian soldier shouted a message to another. What happened next?

NICE SCENERY!

(Clue: It's bury cold.)

2 In 1905 a worker in a pressurised chamber was digging a tunnel under a river in New York. Suddenly the tunnel collapsed – what happened to the worker?

(Clue: Think of a champagne cork.)

WHAT A FALL! YES, WHAT A FOOL!

3 In 1911 stuntman Bobby Leach had just gone over the Niagara Falls in a barrel. The spectators rushed to see what had happened to him. Well?

(Clue: It was a shattering experience.)

4 Scottish scientist Peter Gurthie Tait (1831-1901) was crazy about golf and invented a golf ball that glowed in the dark. What happened to his opponent?

(Clue: There's no smoke without it.)

Answers (total score eight points):

1 The force of the sound waves started avalanches that buried several thousand soldiers.

2 The air in the chamber kept the water out. When the tunnel collapsed the worker was shot upwards by the force of the air and he ended up floating in the river.

3 The force of the buffeting water broke nearly every bone in his body. He recovered, only to die a few months later after slipping on a banana skin.

Forceful sports/pastimes quiz

Simply match the missing words to the sport. Just to make it a bit harder there's a question where we haven't given you the word. (You'll have to work this word out for yourself.)

Missing words

a) tights

b) steep sides

c) springy steel

d) sheep guts

1 Weightlifters use _____ to help them lift weights.

2 In the 1920s US racetracks had _____ sides to make the cars drive faster.

3 Cyclists wear _____ or shave their legs to increase their speed by up to 10 per cent.

4 Traditional tennis rackets got their springiness from _____ .

5 In the world cow-pat-hurling championships the rules say that cow pats can't be moulded to reduce drag. Drag is the force of the _____ hitting the moving object.

Answers (total score five points):

1 c) Weightlifters first lift the bar up to chest level. When the weights on the ends of the springy steel bar spring upwards the movement helps the weight to be raised more easily.

2 b) The cars had to be fast. If they slowed to under 99 km (110 miles per hour) they fell down the steep sides of the track under the influence of gravity.

YOU FORGOT TO PUT THE PETROL CAP BACK ON

SPLOSH!

3 a) Cyclists try to be as streamlined as possible to reduce drag.

4 d) It took seven dead sheep to make one racket. Can ewe believe it?

IT TAKES GUTS TO PLAY THIS GAME!

5 The missing word is AIR. Fancy a few hours moulding cow poo? By the way, the rules also state that the cow pats must be 100 per cent poo. So you need a breath of fresh air? You're just about to get one!

Dare you discover ... the power of air?

What you need:

A straw

A full bottle of your favourite drink. (You certainly need bottle for this experiment.)

A large blob of blu-tak

What you do:

1 Open the bottle and insert the straw.

2 Mould the blu-tak around the straw so that it completely blocks the opening and hold it in position.

3 Try to drink without taking your lips away from the straw.

What do you notice?

a) The drink rises up the straw without being sucked.

b) It gets harder and harder to suck anything up.

c) I started dribbling uncontrollably.

Answer (five points):
b) Normally you start by sucking air from the straw and your mouth. The force of the air pushing down on the drink then pushes the drink up through the straw and into your mouth. But if the air can't get into the bottle this doesn't happen.

The awfully small atoms quiz

This is a MORE or LESS quiz. All you have to do is say MORE or LESS to each question.

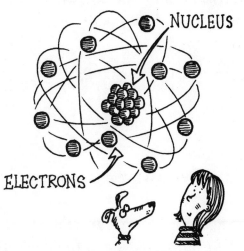
NUCLEUS

ELECTRONS

Here's some info to get you started...

Everything in the universe including you is made of atoms. Each atom consists of a tiny ball of matter called the nucleus surrounded by blips of energy called electrons. The largest atoms are just 0.5 *millionths* of a millimetre across.

1 If an atom was the size of an international football stadium the nucleus would be the size of a tennis ball. MORE/LESS?

2 The electrons would be the size of mosquitoes. MORE/LESS?

3 If you were the size of an atom, a pebble would be the size of the Earth. MORE/LESS?

4 In one second your hair grows the length of one atom. MORE/LESS?

5 Three atoms would stretch across the liquid wall that encloses an air bubble. MORE/LESS?

Answers (total score five points):

1 LESS. It would be the size of a marble – and yes, atoms are a waste of space!

2 MORE. Well, a bit. They would be as big as flies buzzing around the outer walls.

3 MORE. It would be the *twice* the size of the Earth!

4 MORE. It grows the length of 20 atoms!

5 MORE. The wall of an air bubble is one thousandth of a millimetre – the width of over 2,000 atoms.

Buzzing and blazing

This section is all about electricity and light – buzzing and blazing – geddit? You may be interested to know that an electrical current is made of electrons. And electrons actually make light too. Light, in the form of blips of energy (called photons), is given out by electrons when they heat up.

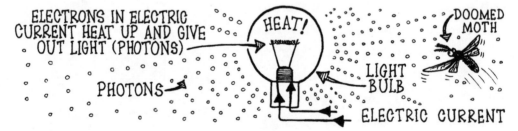

ELECTRONS IN ELECTRIC CURRENT HEAT UP AND GIVE OUT LIGHT (PHOTONS)

HEAT!

DOOMED MOTH

PHOTONS

LIGHT BULB

ELECTRIC CURRENT

Oh well, that's the Science lesson over...

Shocking electric wordsearch

This quiz asks you to find and draw a line through words hidden in the table on the next page. The words you'll be looking for are the ones written in CAPITALS in the shocking facts opposite...

1 In 1999 2,000 British rail travellers and 14 trains were held up by a metal foil yoghurt POT LID. The lid had got stuck in a crack on the electric rail and diverted the electric current into the ground. Of course, without power the trains were stuck.

2 The PAUL TRAP is an arrangement of electric and magnetic forces that traps atoms between them so that they can't get lost and can be studied at leisure. It was invented by German scientist Wolfgang Paul in 1989.

3 In 1750 physicist William Watson performed an experiment. He made a line of people hold hands linking an electricity-making machine with a CANNON. An electric current passed along the line and everyone got an electric shock.

4 During a sandstorm electric force is made by bits of SAND rubbing together. One German explorer caught in a sandstorm wore a CAR JACK (a tool for lifting up cars) on his head with a lead to the ground. The jack attracted the electric force and the lead diverted it to the ground – just like a lightning conductor.

5 One of the earliest electric inventions was meant to catch the Loch Ness MONSTER. It was designed to electrify the water and kill the poor beastie, but luckily this cruel invention never got off the drawing board. Nessie lives!

6 Lightning is a giant electric spark made by thunderstorms. A bolt of lightning can actually make fertilizer – the HEAT of the lightning causes a chemical reaction in the soil that makes NITRIC ACID. Further reactions turn the acid into chemicals called nitrates that plants need so they can grow.

Wordsearch

The words can appear the right way round, backwards, from top to bottom or bottom to top. *(One point per word, total score 12 points.)*

```
D  C  I  R  T  I  N  O
I  A  E  N  A  C  N  A
L  R  E  T  S  N  O  M
T  H  E  A  T  A  N  A
O  T  E  H  S  A  N  D
P  A  R  T  L  U  A  P
K  C  A  J  D  I  C  A
```

Bonus question

Lightning never strikes twice in the same place: TRUE OR FALSE?

> ### Answer (two points):
> FALSE. In 1899 a man in Toronto, Canada was killed by lightning in his backyard. In 1929 his son was killed by lightning in the same spot and can you guess what happened to his grandson in 1949?
>
>

I reckon they could have done with a lightning conductor. Its inventor, Benjamin Franklin (1706-1790), was an electrical science superstar who developed the theory of electric charges and lots more besides. Here's your chance to get clued up on this fascinating scientist.

Benjamin Franklin's puzzling pictures quiz

In this quiz you're shown pictures of the answers but they're muddled up and you'll have to match the answers to the questions correctly. Here's an example question to show you how it's done.

QUESTION

Franklin thought it was healthy to sit by an open window in winter without any of his...?

DESCRIPTION

Answer: Clothing.

(Don't try this at home. It's not very comfortable and it's probably against the law!)

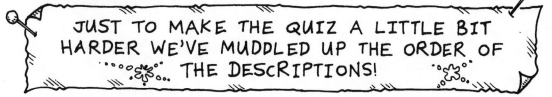

JUST TO MAKE THE QUIZ A LITTLE BIT HARDER WE'VE MUDDLED UP THE ORDER OF THE DESCRIPTIONS!

QUESTIONS

1 When Franklin lived in London he enjoyed a dip in the local...?

2 One of Franklin's most popular inventions was a...?

3 Franklin organised a competition to develop a food that would result in a sweet smelling...?

4 In 1755 Franklin got on his horse and chased a...?

5 Franklin was a key figure in the struggle to make the USA independent of Britain. He suggested the American symbol should be a...?

DESCRIPTIONS

a) TORNADO

b) RIVER

c) ROCKING CHAIR

d) TURKEY

e) FART

DON'T FORGET TO WORK OUT THE ANSWERS FROM THE DESCRIPTIONS!

Answers (total score five points):

1 b) RIVER. The Thames was full of dead cats, rats and floating poo so so swimming in it was almost like committing sewer-cide. Franklin also enjoyed writing letters in the bath (no doubt when he was trying to get clean afterwards).

2 c) ROCKING CHAIR. Does that make Franklin a rocking roll star?

3 e) FARTS. The competition might have been nothing to sniff at but it failed to find a winner.

4 a) TORNADO. He hit the tornado with his whip but it just whipped around as usual.

5 d) TURKEY. Do you reckon the USA would be such a powerful nation today if its national symbol was a *turkey*?

Bonus question

Who did Benjamin Franklin describe as:

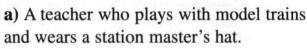

THE SADDEST PERSON IN THE WORLD?

CHOO CHOO!

a) A teacher who plays with model trains and wears a station master's hat.

DERR!

b) A lonely man on a rainy day who doesn't know how to read.

GLOOM! DESPAIR!

c) A school pupil on a Monday morning.

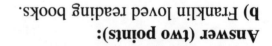

Answer (two points):
b) Franklin loved reading books.

34

Bonus question

Why is it hard to get acne in the Antarctic? (Clue: You'll take a shine to this fact.)

a) High energy ultraviolet light kills the acne germs.

b) The snow is good for your skin.

c) It's hard to find warm water so people don't wash and the build-up of dirt cures the acne.

> **Answer (two points):**
> **a)** Ultraviolet is an invisible type of light that's harmful to human skin and germs – so using it to get rid of acne might be a little rash – geddit? Because of a hole in the ozone layer that protects most of the Earth from this light you'll get more ultraviolet in Antarctica – good for spots, bad for the environment.

So how did you get on?

Well, you've got through this chapter and I bet you're wondering how you're getting on! Are you full of physics facts ... or do you feel a physics flop?

Here's what your score means...

SCOREBOARD

Less than **8** SHOCKING | **8-30** A LIGHT score | **31-55** FORCEFUL | **55+** ELECTRIFYING!

Mind you, whilst we're on the subject of light, the only reason that we know there's a universe out there at all is because telescopes detect light from objects in space. So why don't you *rocket* on to the next chapter? It's awesome!

NEXT CHAPTER

Awesome astronomy

As you know, astronomy is the branch of Science that deals with outer space and its stars and planets and moons and asteroids and galaxies and black holes and, well, everything really. Astronomy is an AWFULLY BIG subject and here are a few facts that your teacher won't know in ten billion trillion light years. Here's a friendly astronomer to set the scene...

HORRIBLE SCIENCE PROFILES 3

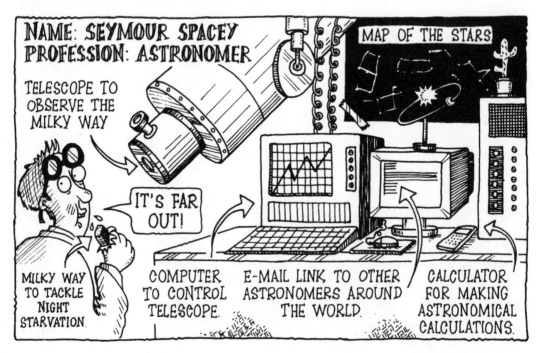

Here's me in the observatory where I work, but astronomers like me don't do much star gazing. That's because our observatories are controlled by computers that do the job for us. This makes life easy because we can actually go to sleep most nights! Another aspect of the job I like is visiting observatories all over the world and swapping info with my fellow astronomers. Yes, this job's really out of this world!

Astonishing astronomers questions and answers quiz

The astronomers of the past were an astonishing bunch – just train your telescope on these questions and match each to the right answer.

QUESTIONS

1 In 1871 French astronomer Pierre Jansenn (1828-1907) was trapped in Paris during a siege. What did he do?

2 Why did Professor James Challis (1803-1882) fail to discover the planet Neptune?

3 How did German-born scientist Hans Bethe find out how the sun works?

4 Why might you find businessman James Lick at the observatory that bears his name?

5 What happened to science superstar Galileo Galilei (1564-1642) 200 years *after* he died.

6 Why did German scientist Erwin Freundlich miss an eclipse of the sun?

ANSWERS

a) SOMEONE STOLE HIS BONES.

b) HE WAS ARRESTED AS A SPY.

c) HIS DEAD BODY IS BURIED THERE.

d) HE WENT FOR A FLIGHT IN A BALLOON.

e) HE DRANK A CUP OF TEA.

f) HE WROTE HIS CALCULATIONS ON THE BACK OF AN ENVELOPE.

Answers (total score six points):

1 d) Pierre Jansenn wanted to see an eclipse of the sun (that's when the moon gets between the sun and the Earth) which could only be seen from North Africa, but he was trapped in Paris. He risked death to escape but when he got to North Africa it was too cloudy to see anything.

2 e) The British Professor was having a cup of tea and a chat with a fellow astronomer. German scientist Johann Encke also missed out because he was at a party, and so his assistants Johann Galle and Heinrich D'Arrest grabbed the glory.

3 f) Hans was on a train when he realized that the sun makes heat and light through fusing hydrogen atoms together to make helium. I expect he was really chuff-chuffed.

4 c) James Lick (1796-1876) is buried in the Californian observatory. I expect he wanted a tomb with a view.

5 a) Galileo was the first scientist to use a telescope to study the planets but an Italian priest opened his tomb and stole a few of his bones as souvenirs in 1737.

6 b) The German astronomer had gone to Russia to observe an eclipse of the sun and find out if megastar scientist Albert Einstein was right when he suggested that the sun's gravity could bend light from distant stars. But World War I broke out and all the scientist saw was the inside of a cell!

Bonus question

Why was the mum of German astronomer Johannes Kepler (1571-1631) arrested as a witch?

a) She *was* a witch.

b) Her son wrote a science fiction novel in which he said she was a witch.

c) People thought her son's telescope had magical powers.

Answer (two points):

b) In 1610 Kepler wrote the world's first science fiction novel in which his mum starred as a witch. The poor old woman was thought to be a real witch and she was arrested and threatened with torture but Kepler got her released.

PHEW!

Did you notice back there we were talking about Albert Einstein? You may not be sure what Einstein actually discovered but don't worry. There are plenty of people who have *studied* Einstein and are still **not** sure what he discovered! In fact, Einstein's work has shaped our entire view of the universe and how it works. Albert Einstein (1879-1955) developed the General Theory of Relativity. This showed that space is curved and that time is actually a dimension of space. Got all that?

Anyway, this quiz is a bit easier.

Albert Einstein's picture-this quiz

All you have to do in this quiz is identify the answers from the pictures. It's that easy (or maybe not!).

1 What were Albert's first words about?
2 On what grounds was Albert rejected for military service?
3 What did Einstein describe as:

THE HAPPIEST THOUGHT OF MY LIFE

4 What did he call:

MY MOST IMPORTANT ITEM OF SCIENTIFIC EQUIPMENT

5 What was Albert's favourite hobby?

6 What simple mistake did Albert make in his Theory of Relativity?

POSSIBLE ANSWERS

a) WASTEPAPER BASKET

b) VIOLIN

c) FLAT FEET AND VARICOSE VEINS

d) BEING WEIGHTLESS IN A LIFT FALLING DOWN A LIFT SHAFT

e) DIVIDING A FIGURE BY ZERO

f) HIS SOUP BEING TOO HOT

Answers (total score six points):

1 f) Albert was four when he spoke for the first time. When asked why he hadn't spoken earlier he said, "Because up until now everything was in order".

2 c) This was lucky because Albert was anti-war and would have refused to join the army.

3 d) This thought led him to the Theory of Relativity – just don't ask me to explain how.

4 a) The wastepaper bin was valuable because Albert learnt from his mistakes. Perhaps you could try throwing your homework in the bin and quoting this fact to your teacher?

5 b) Einstein enjoyed playing the violin and he was a *relatively* talented musician, ha ha.

6 e) Any Maths teacher can tell you that it's impossible to divide anything by zero. This fact was pointed out by Russian mathematician Alexander Friedman (1885-1925).

Now you've got a handle on general relativity you might just fancy seeing it in action and exploring outer space. OK, so how about becoming an astronaut?

Spaced-out space travel quiz

IN THIS QUIZ YOU NEED TO ADD THE MISSING WORDS TO THE SPACE MANUAL. (OH, AND JUST TO SPACE YOU OUT, THERE'S A COUPLE OF SPARE WORDS THAT YOU WON'T NEED.)

Here are the missing words...

a) eyeballs, **b)** beans, **c)** golf course, **d)** germs (bacteria), **e)** lucky toy rabbit, **f)** sick, **g)** vicar, **h)** paint, **i)** jet plane, **j)** litter, **k)** camera, **l)** passport

And here's the space manual...

THE HORRIBLE SCIENCE SPACE TRAVEL GUIDE

INTRODUCTION

So you want to be an astronomer? C-o-o-l! It's an out of this world job! But it's also a tad dangerous, so don't start complaining if you get killed!!!

TREMBLE!

Chapter 1: TRAINING

You'll have to train for years before we let you near our lovely expensive rockets. The first bit is getting used to being weightless in space. We train you for this by taking you up in a

(1) _____ and diving at speed. You'll be weightless for a few seconds and think you're going to crash and die. Don't worry – we'll only be doing this 40 times a day. Then there's the jungle survival course – 'cos you never know where you might land!

ERK!

Hiss!

Chapter 2: **READY TO TAKE OFF?**

Remember not to start your rocket before the end of the countdown. Oops, nearly forgot! Don't forget your (2) _____. As I said, you never know where you might land!

Chapter 3: **LIVING IN SPACE**

You might feel unwell – this is because your weightless body is confused and doesn't know which way up it is. Hopefully you won't feel too unwell – we don't want weightless (3) _____ floating about. It's hard to wash without water floating everywhere so our advice is *don't*. And don't wash your clothes – your parents can do your laundry when you get back to Earth. By the way, you shouldn't apply to be an astronaut to avoid taking a bath!

Chapter 4: **SPACE WALKING**

You might need to do repair work on a satellite. Remember to put on your space suit before you go outside. Without a suit, your guts and then your (4) _____ will explode. Now that's what I call atmos–fear! Oh, and don't go locking yourself out by mistake – it's a long way for the fire brigade to come and rescue you! Try not to knock the satellite off course. Some astronauts did this in 1996 and lost $44 million of high-tech equipment. And bits of lost satellite can turn up in embarrassing places; in 1979 one landed on a **(5)** _____ in Eastbourne, England.

Chapter 5: BEWARE OF SPACE JUNK

When you're working outside watch out for space junk whizzing around the Earth at high speeds. A lump the size of a marble can fly through your body and come out the other side! The space-shuttle *Challenger* was hit by a fleck of **(6)** _____ that dented its front window. Look out for the **(7)** _____ dropped by US astronaut Michael Collins, and the glove dropped by Russian cosmonaut Aleksei Leonov in 1965 – they're both whizzing around somewhere up there.

Chapter 6: EXPERIMENTS

Living in space can be boring – so why not keep animals in space? A swarm of bees got used to weightlessness and built their own hive – and the astronauts got a real buzz too. Astronauts have also grown oats and **(8)** _____ .

Chapter 7: VISITING THE MOON

In 1967 a robot spacecraft left a camera on the moon which was later fetched by astronauts. Scientists found the camera casing contained dried snot with living **(9)** _____ . Try not to leave **(10)** _____ as there's already over 50 tonnes on the moon left over from visits in the 1970s.

Answers (total score ten points):

1 i) The astronauts are weightless because their bodies aren't resisting gravity. (What we call "weight" is simply the measure of how much gravity pulls on our bodies.)

2 l) Astronauts carry passports. After all, you might land in a foreign country or an alien planet.

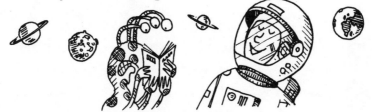

3 f) If you want to complain about living in space you could always travel by *moan*-rocket, ha ha.

4 a) The air in the body pushes outwards with the same pressure as the air pushes inwards on the body. Because there's no air in space the air in the body explodes. This could be a sight for sore eyes.

5 c) The bit of satellite landed on a golf course and I suppose it made a hole in one.

6 h)

7 k) At least he didn't lose a sausage – then it would have become a UFO (unidentified frying object).

8 b) The plants grew normally although some roots went up instead of down. If the plants had died they would have become "has beans".

9 d) Bacteria – yes, they *can* live on the Moon (although they weren't growing or multiplying). Scientists believe that bacteria can also survive in space.

10 j) The litter includes six landers and three lunar rovers. (Lunar rovers are space vehicles – not pet moon-dogs.)

THIS SORT

NOT THIS SORT

Could YOU boldly go where not too many people have been before?

So how do you use a space toilet? Here are the stages involved, just put them in the right order. Any mistakes and you'll be covered in unmentionable substances. (You can have one point for each stage listed in the right order.)

WARNING: this quiz is a bit rude so don't leave it on your granny's chair!

a) Don't forget to wipe the toilet and your nether regions using a special wipe.

b) Sit down on the toilet seat.

c) Switch on the fan to suck the poo and pee out of the base of the toilet otherwise it will splurge all over you.

d) Grip the handles on either side to stop your body floating off the loo at a vital moment.

e) Connect your vital bits and pieces to the right-sized funnel or nozzle and … NO, I'm *not* going into details.

f) Press the button to increase the suction for poo.

Answers (total score six points):
First b), second e), third d), fourth c), fifth f), sixth a). Still wanna be an astronaut?

45

The stunning solar system

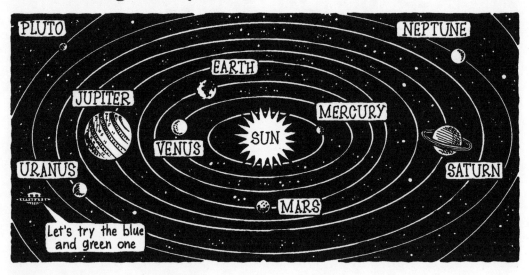

Solar system wordsearch

Remember the wordsearch on page 32? Here's another one. The words you'll be looking for this time are the ones written in CAPITALS in the other-worldly facts below.

1 RADAR is a method of bouncing radio waves off an object. This technique has been used to "see" through the clouds of Venus and make maps of its surface that are better than maps of the Earth.

2. On JUPITER you'll find the great red spot – a huge storm three times larger than planet Earth.

3 The rings of SATURN become invisible every 14 years. That's because the rings tilt with the planet but we can't see them when they're end-on to Earth.

4 The volcanoes on IO erupt so much rock that the moon turns inside-out every 10,000 years.

5 Another of Jupiter's moons, EUROPA, is covered in ice that could hide a deep ocean of water in which alien life forms might lurk. Fancy a dip?

6 US astronomer Percival Lowell (1855-1916) reckoned he'd discovered alien canals on MARS. The markings were also spotted by Italian scientist Giovanni Schiaparelli (1835-1910) in 1877 but he thought they were natural features.

7 The largest crater on the MOON is the size of Scotland – that's 67,300 square km (or 26,000 square miles) – but you probably won't find an alien haggis there.

Wordsearch *(One point per word, total score seven points.)*

```
N S G N I R
R A N S R E
U P O I A T
T O O S D I
A R M R A P
S U N A R U
R E A M A J
```

Bonus question
American astronomer David Levi said:

> JUPITER IS THE SOLAR
> SYSTEM'S VACUUM CLEANER.

What on Earth – or rather, what on Jupiter does he mean?
a) Jupiter hoovers the solar system free of dust.
b) Jupiter runs off electricity and its power can be controlled.
c) Jupiter sucks in comets and stops them from hitting us.

Answer (two points):
c) Yes – Jupiter's gravity sucks in comets. If it wasn't for Jupiter we'd have been flattened by a comet and wiped out long ago!

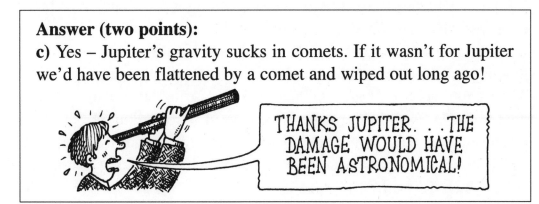

> THANKS JUPITER. . .THE
> DAMAGE WOULD HAVE
> BEEN ASTRONOMICAL!

Awful expressions

An astronomer says:

I STUDY BLUE STRAGGLER STARS

Do you say…?

a) Cool. The Blue Stragglers are the best pop group ever!

b) They're stars that move more slowly than the others and look a bit sad and pathetic. That's why they're called blue stragglers.

c) Nasty blighters – heaven help us if they ever come near our solar system.

Answer (one point):

c) Blue straggler stars are the biggest bullies of the galaxy. They bump into other stars and then orbit them, sucking in gases from the weaker star through the force of gravity and getting bigger and brighter.

The amazing universe quiz

Here are some amazing universe facts which no teacher in the solar system will know. Which facts are just too amazing to be true? Answer TRUE or FALSE.

1 When scientists discovered heat energy from the Big Bang – the huge explosion that happened at the beginning of time when the universe started to expand – they thought it was made by aliens.

2 Our galaxy contains millions of diamonds floating around in space.

3 Formalin has been found in space. (This is true, but what about the next bit?) On Earth this chemical is found in school dinners.

4 Astronomers have discovered alcohol floating around in space.

5 All the gold on Earth was made in exploding stars long before the solar system formed.

Answers (total score five points):

1 FALSE. The scientists working for the US Bell Laboratories in 1964 detected microwaves made by rapidly moving blips of heat energy given out by cooling gas after the Big Bang. But they thought the signals were interference caused by pigeon poo on their radar telescope and spent ages cleaning it before they realized that the pigeons were innocent.

2 TRUE. The Milky Way is full of diamonds. (That's our galaxy I'm talking about – not the choccie bar.) There's about one billion tonnes of diamonds just floating around up there – enough to make an entire planet! They're actually the remains of exploded stars.

3 FALSE. (Hopefully.) Formalin is used by undertakers to preserve dead bodies. It's poisonous – so you wouldn't want to taste it even if you fancied a "stiff" drink.

4 TRUE. There's enough alcohol in a typical chemical cloud in space to make 10,000,000,000,000,000,000,000,000 (ten million billion billion) bottles of whisky.

5 TRUE. Gold is formed when stars explode.

So how did you get on?

So you've toured the universe and studied the solar system – but have you returned talking like a science star or an aimless alien?
Here's what your score means...

SCOREBOARD

Less than **10** ECLIPSED
10-25 SPACED-OUT
26-39 ASTRONOMICAL
40+ COSMIC!

Mind you, all those substances knocking about in space have one thing in common. They're all chemicals, and that means they'll be of interest to the scientists in the next chapter. Know what I'm getting at? It's time to crack open those test tubes!

Chaotic chemistry

Chemists study chemicals and chemical reactions – that's how chemicals change if you mix them up or alter their temperature. So if you want to chatter to a chemist you'd best sharpen up your reactions – and who better to provide the low-down than a genuine chaotic chemist...

HORRIBLE SCIENCE PROFILES 4

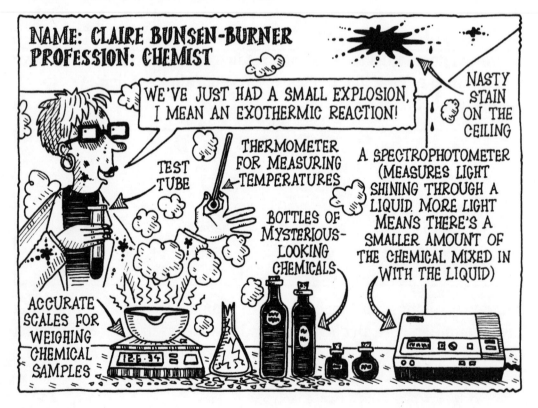

Chemistry is cool! Look around your home and you'll see washing powders and soap and disinfectant and paints and dyes — in other words, chemicals! And wherever chemicals are made, there are chemists testing and mixing the substances and developing new mixtures. We chemists pop up everywhere! Me, I'm working for a cosmetics firm in quality control — that means I get to test the chemicals in the make-up and shampoo to make sure they've been mixed properly. I get loads of free samples too!

And talking about mixing – it's time to mix with a few quizzes.

Spot that substance!

Here's a collection of chemicals. All you need to do is work out which question each one appears in.

Substances

a) DIAMOND
b) OZONE GAS
c) IRON PYRITE
e) GOLD
d) VANILLALDEHYDE
f) METHYL MERCAPTAN
(ME-THILE MARE-CAP-TAN)
g) SOOT

1 This substance is so easy to roll flat that you could melt a lump the size of a matchbox and use it to cover a tennis court.

2 In this substance you'll find bucky onions and bucky bunnies. These are balls of carbon atoms and (believe it or not) bucky onions actually have layers like onions and bucky bunnies have "ears" like rabbits! Finding them must have been a hare-raising discovery.

3 In 1905 British King Edward VII was given a present of this substance and said:

I SHOULD HAVE KICKED IT ASIDE AS A LUMP OF GLASS HAD I SEEN IT UPON THE ROAD.

4 German chemist Christian Schönbein (1799-1868) discovered this substance after he noticed a nasty smell in his laboratory.

5 In 1578 explorer Martin Frobisher (1535-1594) risked his life to bring back this substance from the north of Canada thinking it was gold – it wasn't.

THIS GOLD IS LIKE SEAWATER

WHAT DO YOU MEAN?

THERE'S GALLEONS OF IT ALL AROUND US!

6 Just a pinch of this substance can pong out an entire sports stadium. (Clue: The chemical is also found in the flavouring of certain ice-creams.)

7 The human body makes this substance from chemicals in asparagus and it makes the pee really whiffy. In the Second World War US pilots were given asparagus soup to eat if they were shot down. The pilots were told to pee in the sea and catch fish attracted by the smell.

YOU'RE KIDDING!

Answers (total score seven points):

1 e) Actually, if you piled all the gold that has ever been found into a square block it could still fit inside that tennis court.

2 g) The first carbon balls to be found were buckyballs (see page 54).

3 a) In 1905 Edward was given the world's largest diamond as a birthday present. Natural diamonds actually look like glass – it's only when they're cut that they really shine.

4 b) Ozone means "I smell" in Greek. The chemical, which normally takes the form of a gas, had been produced by a chemical reaction triggered by a powerful electrical current. And yes, this is the same gas that protects us from ultra-violet rays (see page 35).

5 c) Iron pyrite is also known as "fool's gold". "I'm galled," as Martin might have said – but at least the pyrite made a useful road-building material.

6 d) The chemical is a concentrated form of vanilla flavouring.

7 f) The chemical is methyl mercaptan (me-thile mare-cap-tan) – said to be the most disgusting smell in the world. It reeks of rotten cabbage, garlic, onions, burnt toast and stinking blocked toilets.

Fancy a sniff?

Awful atoms (again)

Chemicals are made of atoms and we need to revisit their chaotic world to learn a new word. A molecule is a group of atoms that have joined in a chemical reaction to form a particular chemical. Got all that?

Molecule more or less quiz

This is a MORE or LESS quiz and you should be more or less sure of the rules by now. All you do is say MORE or LESS to each question.

1 It takes six million atoms to fill a thimble. MORE or LESS?

2 In just one teaspoonful of water there are as many molecules as there are teaspoonfuls of water in a full bath. (Don't start counting them now.) MORE or LESS?

53

3 Every second your body falls apart. Well, four billion atoms in your body fall apart – these atoms are radioactive and that means that they're too heavy and simply fall apart to form other substances. MORE or LESS?

4 Bucky balls are a type of carbon similar to bunny balls. They're so bouncy that you can throw one at a steel wall at 50 kilometres (31 miles) per hour and it will *still* bounce back rather than splatting flat like a bug on a windscreen. MORE or LESS?

5 The air in Los Angeles smells of hot dogs (the only dogs that feed the hand that bites them). In fact, the smells are made of molecules of meat floating around and the combined weight of these molecules is the same as 200 elephants. MORE or LESS?

Answers (total score five points):

1 MORE. It takes 600,000,000,000,000,000,000,000,000 (six hundred thousand billion billion) atoms to fill a thimble. They weigh as much as a thimbleful of water – after all, that thimbleful of water is just a load of old atoms!

2 MORE. If you split up all the molecules in a drop of water and stir them into the sea you'll end up with 24 of your original molecules in every 0.6 litres (or one pint) of sea water. That means that there are as many molecules in that teaspoon of water as there are teaspoonfuls of water in the Atlantic Ocean.

3 LESS. It's only 400,000 – and don't worry, this *isn't* fatal and only involves one in every 225 million of your atoms.

4 MORE. We're talking 27,400 km (17,000 miles) per hour and it will still bounce back.

5 LESS. It's only four elephants. Mind you, it's lucky no one's frying elephant burgers.

Awful expressions
A scientist says:

I WEIGH MOLES

Do you say…?

a) So what – I once weighed my pet hamster.

b) Oh – so you study atomic weight?

c) Molecules Of Lumpy Elastic Substances – hmm, fascinating.

Answer (one point):
b) A mole is a way of comparing the weights of a sample of atoms with 12 grams (0.42 ounces) of a type of carbon. You can't weigh a single atom because no one has a small enough set of scales.

Crucial chemicals quiz

A nice, straightforward quiz – well, if you get it right! All you have to do is match each product with its ingredient. Can you sort them out?

PRODUCTS

1 Fencing rapiers (swords used in the sport of fencing – that's sword fighting and nothing to do with garden fencing) and jet planes are made from...

2 Roman toothpaste was made from...

3 Victorian hats contained...

4 Fertilizers contain...

5 Ancient Egyptian glue was made from...

6 Toilet paper is made using...

7 Artificial limbs are made using...

8 Pencil lead contains...

9 In the 1870s some chewing gum contained ...

10 In Victorian times the centres of golf balls contained...

INGREDIENTS

a) CHEESE

b) POISONOUS MERCURY

c) A SUBSTANCE FOUND IN ROTTEN BIRD'S POO AND DEAD FISH

d) SULPHURIC ACID

e) HONEY

f) SEAWEED

g) PARAFFIN

h) A STRONG ALLOY (MIXTURE OF METALS) CALLED KEVLAR

i) CLAY

j) PEE

Answers (total score ten points):

1 h) Kevlar has two uses – jets and fencing swords. It must be a duel-purpose material.

2 j) Ammonia is a chemical found in pee and was used in Roman times to make toothpaste. Containers were placed on street corners for people to pee in. They flushed and you brushed.

3 b) Mercury was used to stiffen hats. The poisonous chemical caused madness – hence the saying "mad as a hatter".

4 c) Fertilizers contain phosphates. The island of Nauru in the Pacific Ocean is built on phosphate made from the remains of half-rotted bird poo and dead fish – fancy a holiday there?

5 a) The ancient Egyptians used cheesy substances as glue. They mixed whey from milk with lime to make the glue. In the 1800s it was found that in damp conditions the glue turned into cheesy gunge. Throw that away and even your bin will get indigestion.

6 d) Sulphuric acid (yes – the same acid that's found on Venus) is used to make the stiff "medicated" type of loo paper see-through. The paper is dipped in acid but the acid is washed off afterwards otherwise it would burn yer bum.

7 f) Artificial limbs are made out of plastic but they sometimes contain chemicals made from seaweed.

8 i) Clay is an ingredient of pencil "lead". The clay is mixed with graphite (yet another form of carbon) and baked for hardness.

9 g) Paraffin is a type of fuel oil. By gum – it must have tasted disgusting!

10 e) What a sweet idea!

Bonus question

Which of these products does NOT include seaweed?

a) Headache pills

b) Light bulbs

c) Shaving cream

Answer (two points):
b) But seaweed IS used to help make them. It's used to make the tungsten wire more slippery so that it can be lengthened to make the filament (the little wire inside the bulb).

Chemical hoax quiz

If these stories appeared on 1 April which of them would be April Fool hoaxes? Answer FALSE if you think the story is a hoax. Otherwise, answer TRUE.

Try this quiz on a friend and don't forget to shout "April Fool!" when they get an answer wrong!

1

US Air Force News 1970

AIR FORCE SCENTS VICTORY

The US Air Force Aeronautical Services Division has experimented PING! with using smells as weapons.

A spokesperson said, "We cannot confirm or deny this story," but added, "There's definitely something in the air."

2

FRENCH DYE NEWS
···❈·· 1859 ·❈····

COLOURFUL REMINDER OF BLOODY BATTLE

The newly-invented blood-red/purple dye is to be named Magenta in memory of the recent Battle of Magenta. Emperor Napoleon III says "Whilst our soldiers were dying the chemists were dyeing and now they're dying to give their dye this name!"

3

THE SAN FRANCISCO TIMES - 1999

CHEESY SURPRISE FOR TASTEFUL DINNER

Scientists have discovered how to make the cheesy whiff of old socks into a new food flavouring. A scientist said "It's safe, it's cheap, it's healthy and it's hard cheese for anyone who doesn't like it."

4

THE CONFEDERATE NEWS - 1864

PEE FOR VICTORY!

We might be short of gunpowder in this great American Civil War but your pee contains nitrates and we can use these chemicals to make saltpetre – a vital gunpowder ingredient. So give your pee to the war effort – every pot-ful makes a pot-shot!

5

THE CHOCOHOLIC MAGAZINE 2000

MY CHOCOLATE TASTES OF SPINACH!

Scientists have found that chocolate gets some of its taste from a chemical also found in spinach. Parents and teachers are now offering children spinach bars.

6

THE HOUSEBUILDERS' TIMES - 1987

IT'S SOGGY CARDBOARD TO THE RESCUE

German chemists have found that soggy cardboard and gravel can be used as a building material. Said one builder: "We thought the idea was a bit wet but the evidence is solid enough."

7

WHAT BARBECUE?

SCIENTIST BLEW UP MY BARBIE! 1996

An American electronics technician has blown up a barbecue in a failed experiment to see whether liquid oxygen could be used as a fuel. Shocked George Goble said afterwards: "I'm devastated – I really fancied a nice banger."

Answers (total score seven points):

1 TRUE. Groups of people from all over the world have been tested to discover which smells they find most disgusting. For example, the Karen people of Burma hate the smell of cooking fat ... they were going to test the smell of school dinners on children but the test was banned for cruelty.

2 TRUE. The dye was invented by French chemists in 1859.

3 APRIL FOOL! And don't believe the rumour that it's used in school dinners!

4 TRUE. Chocolate contains oxalic acid – the same substance that gives spinach its bitter taste. Chocolate is also naturally bitter but the added sugar prevents you from noticing. What would you rather find between your teeth – spinach or chocolate?

5 TRUE. During the American Civil War (1861-1865) people were urged to pee in pots and a special wagon went round collecting the precious fluid.

6 APRIL FOOL! This idea just won't stand up.

7 TRUE. Oxygen is the gas in the air that we breathe. It's also the gas in the air that makes things burn easily. So things will burn really quickly when there's pure oxygen around.

Double bonus question (Get this right and you'll get four points!)
In 1999 a British toyshop owner accidentally fell on a canister of helium gas used to fill balloons. The nozzle pierced her body and she swelled up like a balloon.
What happened next?
a) She exploded.
b) The gas was lighter than air so she floated up to the ceiling like a balloon.

c) Her body swelled up but luckily the swelling gradually reduced.

Answer (four points):
c) Her stomach was double its normal size and she feared she would explode. But her body slowly got rid of the gas.

Awful expressions
A chemist says:

WHAT A SUPER-SLURPER!

Do you say:

SLURP!

I CAN MAKE GREAT SLURPING SOUNDS!

Answer (one point):
No, super-slurper was the nickname given to H-spon, a substance invented by US chemists in 1974 that could soak up 1,300 times its own weight in moisture. It could be made into nappies for babies who like big drinks!

Dare you discover ... how soap works?

What you need:

Cooking oil

Soap

A hand (use your own unless someone's offered you a hand, ha ha!).

What you do:

1 Pour a little cold cooking oil into the palm of your hand and rub it in using your fingers.

2 Place your hand under the running tap, rubbing the water over your hand with your fingers.

3 Lather up some soap and once again use your fingers to rub the soap over the hand. Place it under the running tap.

What do you notice?

a) My hand felt less slimy after the water but became slimy after the soap.

b) My hand was still slimy after the water and felt less slimy after the soap.

c) My hand felt cold under the water and hot after the soap had been added.

Answer (two points):

b) Cooking oil contains chemicals (found in all fats) that don't mix with water, so rinsing your hands in water won't remove all the oil. Soap consists of molecules with two ends – one end mixes with water and the other mixes with oil. The soap molecules link the oil to the water and the water washes the soap and oil away.

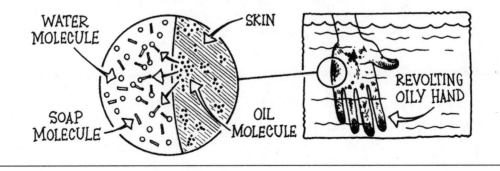

61

Horrible heating

All chemicals on Earth are either in the form of a solid, a liquid or a gas. Take this teacher's cup of tea...

The difference between these "states of matter" (as a chemist would call them) is simply temperature. (Different substances change state at different temperatures.) Got all that?

Now you can get on with the quiz...

Getting in a state quiz

In this quiz each question has *three* possible answers. Gas, liquid or solid. (Surprise, surprise.)

1 Fried eggs stick to pans because the white contains chemicals called proteins. Once the egg is cooked what state is the white in?

2 Cryogenic suspension means preserving dead bodies in very cold nitrogen (a chemical found in air). In what state is the nitrogen?

3 In 1695 a rich nobleman gave two scientists a diamond. As an experiment they heated the gem under a magnifying lens in the sunlight. In what state was the diamond by the end of the experiment?

4 What state is glass in?
Clue: it's not the obvious answer!

5 The height of the Eiffel Tower actually depends on the weather. All metals expand when hot as their atoms try to move apart and the Tower grows by 15 cm (6 inches). In what state is the metal?

6 What state did the lead roof of Washington Cathedral begin to change into in the 1920s?

7 In 1930 five German parachutists jumped into a thundercloud and the cold turned them into human hail. What state were the outside of their bodies?

Answers (total score seven points):

1 Solid. The heated proteins clump together and stick in tiny cracks.

2 Liquid. Nitrogen is normally gas but it becomes a liquid at very cold temperatures. One US cryogenics company hired a site in a cemetery but were chucked out because locals were scared by shadowy figures appearing in the cemetry at night to top up the nitrogen. The bodies ended up in garages and cellars.

3 Gas. It heated and suddenly disappeared in a puff of smoke. Diamonds are actually a form of carbon like coal, and like coal they burn if they're hot enough. Let's hope the nobleman didn't want his diamond back.

4 Liquid. Glass is made of melted sand and other chemicals. Although it might feel solid enough it's actually a very slow moving *liquid*.

5 Solid. The tower stays solid. Mind you, if the tower became too wobbly it might have to be re-named "the Trifle Tower".

6 Liquid. Hot summers were melting the roof. The roof had to be mixed with another chemical, antimony, to raise the temperature at which this effect happened.

7 Solid. A hailstone is made from a frozen water droplet. The droplet grows bigger as more water freezes to it until the air currents in the clouds can't support it and it falls. The parachutists were covered in ice in this way and four were killed. It can't have been an ice way to go.

Bonus question

Some Antarctic fish contain antifreeze in their blood to stop them freezing solid in the cold water. (This is not to be confused with your mum's sister getting stuck in snow – that's auntie-freeze.) The antifreeze chemicals coat ice crystals that form in their blood and stop the crystals from growing. Name two uses for this technology.

Answer (two points):
Scientists hope to use these chemicals to learn how to freeze human body bits for transplants and give ice-cream a smooth texture. Perhaps they could combine the technologies and create body-bit-flavoured ice-cream!

So how did you get on?

So you made it! Congratulations – now all you have to do is to check your score. Here's what it means...

Did someone mention fish a moment ago? Well, whilst we're on the subject, did you know there's a fish that *melts* (or as a chemist might say "changes from a solid to a liquid") in the sun? And if you think that sounds a bit wild, wait till you get to grips with the next brain-pumping chapter.

It's *alive* with horrible facts!

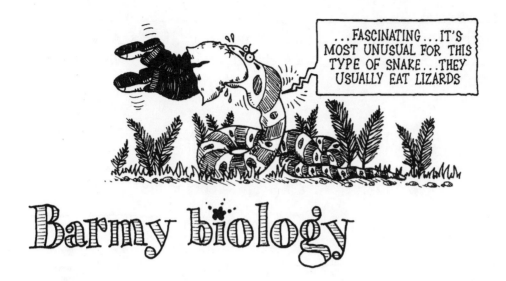

Barmy biology

Biology is the science of living things. Now, I expect you know all about living things – I mean, you're a living thing, and so (allegedly) are your teachers. But like every science subject there's more to biology than meets the eye. Here's a biologist to explain...

HORRIBLE SCIENCE PROFILES 5

Imagine any plant or animal or microbe. If it's alive we want to know how it lives and if it's dead we may want to cut it up and find out what's inside it.

Plant scientists = botanists

Animal scientists = zoologists

Scientists who study how plants and animals live together in an area = ecologists

Me, I'm a flatworm person. I love them and all their fascinating little ways. Did you know you can cut one in half and it becomes two worms? I'm at university studying how a new brain forms in the back end of the worm — fascinating! My idea of a fun day out is to get stuck into a nice, smelly mud flat and study the worms in their natural home.

Actually, some of the life forms you'll be meeting in this chapter aren't as friendly as worms and butterflies. You'll be coming across things that might like to take a bite out of you. And that's just the plants...

Gruesome greenery

A plant is a living thing (usually green) that can use sunlight to transform carbon dioxide gas in the air into food – a trick called photosynthesis (fo-toe-sinth-e-sis). Bug-eating plants also eat insects, and as for the rest, well, a nice drop of blood makes a lovely treat...

Mix your own fertilizer quiz

Choose THREE of the ingredients below and on the next page to make a traditional fertilizer.

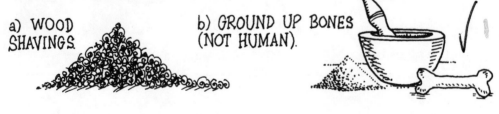

a) WOOD SHAVINGS.

b) GROUND UP BONES (NOT HUMAN).

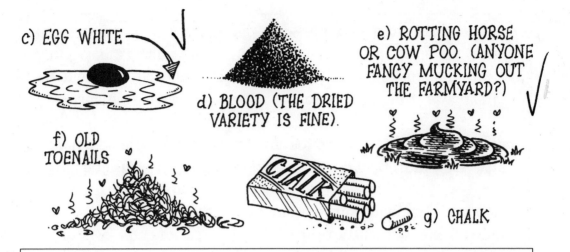

c) EGG WHITE

d) BLOOD (THE DRIED VARIETY IS FINE).

e) ROTTING HORSE OR COW POO. (ANYONE FANCY MUCKING OUT THE FARMYARD?)

f) OLD TOENAILS

g) CHALK

Answer (total score three points):
b), d), e) These substances are rich in chemicals called minerals that plants need to grow strong and healthy. Actually, you need minerals too but you can get minerals from many types of food, so you don't have to eat blood and bones.

Vicious vegetable quiz
All you have to do in this quiz is match the question to its correct answer.

QUESTIONS

1 If you stretched out all the plant roots in a tennis court-sized garden they would cover twice the distance to...? d ✓

2 What makes people stand on the banks of Lake Akan in Japan and stare at the water? a ✓

3 Where is the world's only potato museum? b ✓

4 How did the Feverish Skunk Cabbage get its name? c ✓

5 What helps spider plants grow strong and healthy? e ✓

ANSWERS

a) PLANTS THAT DIVE UP AND DOWN IN THE WATER.

b) BLACKFOOT, IDAHO.

c) THE PLANT IS WARMER THAN ITS SURROUNDINGS.

d) THE MOON.

e) THEY ENJOY A FEW PUFFS OF FORMALIN

Answers (total score five points):
1 d)
2 a) This is a type of duckweed. Like any green plant, it makes food by photosynthesis and gives out oxygen as a by-product. The plants rise when they first produce this oxygen gas and sink after they get rid of it. The sight of all these plants bobbing up and down is a tourist attraction.
3 b) The prize exhibit is a 2000-year-old potato from Peru. Mind you, the potatoes used to make school dinners must be at least that old.
4 c) Chemical reactions in the leaves keep them a few degrees warmer than the surrounding soil and they can even melt snow.
5 e) Scientists aren't too sure why. The chemical is drawn though holes in the plant's leaves and helps the roots grow longer.

Ferocious flowers and foul fruits quiz

Fruits and flowers mean summer days and dainty butterflies. Lazy bumble bees humming around pretty little gardens filled with pansies and kindly old gardeners called Amos pottering around the petunias. Well, that's what you might read in nice little story books – but this is HORRIBLE SCIENCE and this quiz is about stinking fiendish flowers and fruit salad nightmares!

All you have to do is match the plant to the fact. (Just to make it harder one of the facts and one of the plants are MADE UP.)

Plants

1 A TYPE OF AUSTRALIAN MISTLETOE
2 RAFFLESIA
3 BANANA
4 WATER HYACINTH

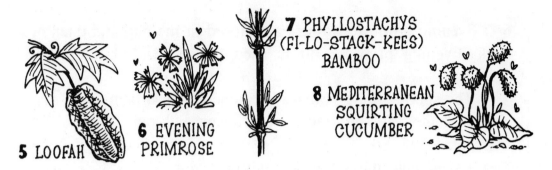

5 LOOFAH
6 EVENING PRIMROSE
7 PHYLLOSTACHYS (FI-LO-STACK-KEES) BAMBOO
8 MEDITERRANEAN SQUIRTING CUCUMBER

Facts

a) It pongs of rotting flesh and attracts flies.

b) This plant grows on trees. It has sticky seeds that stick to a bird's bum.

c) A disaster for lakes. One plant can breed 60,000 more in a few months.

d) It flowers every 120 years.

e) It might splatter you with green slime.

f) Its flowers pop out for the evening.

g) People use this fruit to scratch their backs in the bath.

h) This seedless fruit doesn't grow on trees.

Answers (total score eight points):

1 b) The Australian mistletoe bird eats the seeds and they come out in its poo. The bird then wipes its bum on a tree and the seed can grow on the tree.

2 a) The rafflesia is also known as the "stinking corpse lily". It rots into a black stinking mass and makes a lovely Christmas gift for your teacher.

3 h) Bananas DON'T grow on trees. Bananas are giant plants and the banana fruits are specially bred without seeds so they can be eaten easily. (The black bits inside a banana are the traces of where the seeds should be.)

4 c) Freshwater lakes in many parts of the world are being taken over and choked by the horrible hyacinths.

5 g) Loofahs are a tropical fruit rather like a marrow. The fruit has been dried out to make it hard and scratchy. In the Second World War the fibres in the fruit were used to make padding for helmets.

6 f) Evening primrose flowers are closed in the day and open at dusk. Evening primrose oil is used to treat the skin disease eczema.

7 d) The spooky thing is that every one of these bamboo plants wherever they are on Earth will flower and die at the same moment.

8 e) It's guaranteed to liven up a school dinner.

Could you be an expert on bug-eating plants?

People have found many uses for bug-eating plants. Which of these are genuine? (Choose three.)

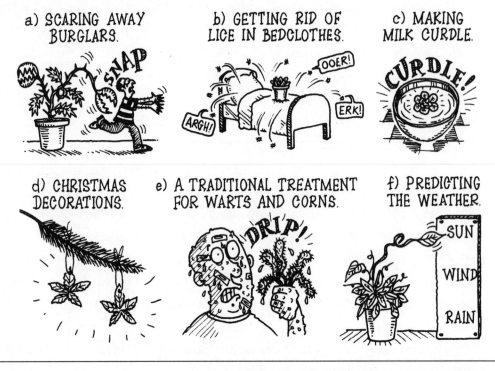

a) SCARING AWAY BURGLARS.

b) GETTING RID OF LICE IN BEDCLOTHES.

c) MAKING MILK CURDLE.

d) CHRISTMAS DECORATIONS.

e) A TRADITIONAL TREATMENT FOR WARTS AND CORNS.

f) PREDICTING THE WEATHER.

Answers (total score three points):

b) The sticky leaves of the Butterwort, a bug-eating plant, were used in many parts of Europe for catching lice in bed.

c) Butterwort juices curdle milk and the curds can be made into cheese.

e) Sundew is another sticky plant and an ointment was made from it's juice. (Unfortunately, it didn't work.)

Murderous microbes and irritating insects

Now it's time to think small, *horribly* small. There are many times more types of insects than all other animals put together and there are probably far more types of microbes than insects...

Incredible bug discoveries quiz

Here are five places that new bugs or microbes have been found – the only problem is that TWO of these places are made up. Which are made up and which are true?

YIKES, I HOPE IT'S NOT b)!

a) Lake Vostock: an underground lake deep beneath the snows of Antarctica.

b) The mouth of a lobster.

c) Deep within an active volcano in Switzerland.

d) On the body of a wasp.

e) Inside the glowing bulb of a sodium street light.

Answers (total score five points):

The made up places are...

c) There are no active volcanoes in Switzerland.

e) The heat of the light would kill any bugs or microbes.

The others are true...

a) Scientists have found strange new types of microbes living in the ice just above the lake and nicknamed them "Mickey Mouse" and "Klingon". The scientists believe that the water may be home to microbes that have been lost to the world for 25 million years.

b) The symbion (sim-be-on), first spotted in 1995, is just 1 mm (0.04 inches) long. In fact, people who eat lobsters have been scoffing the bugs for years without noticing!

d) The xeno (ze-no) is a tiny insect with 100 eyes. Despite all the studies of wasps over the years, no one noticed the xeno until 1995, but I guess the xeno's had its eyes on us.

71

Ugly bug true and false quiz

This is a straightforward quiz – you just say TRUE or FALSE to each question. But there's an ugly twist: for each wrong answer you LOSE a point. For this reason you need someone to read you the quiz and keep note of your score!

1 A magathon is a maggot race organized by the World Organization of Racing Maggots (WORM) at Barney's Bar in Montana, USA. TRUE or FALSE?

2 Insects have been found living on Mars (that's the planet not the chocolate bars). TRUE or FALSE?

3 Blow flies can taste food through their feet. TRUE or FALSE?

4 Mind you, that's nothing – an ichneumon (ick-noy-mon) fly can *hear and smell* through its feet. TRUE or FALSE?

5 The chocolate beetle only eats chocolate. It sneaks into houses and can scoff a whole bar by itself. TRUE or FALSE?

6 Tarantula spiders fire tiny spears at mice. TRUE or FALSE?

7 The sea cucumber is a kind of sea slug that defends itself by squirting its guts over an attacker. TRUE or FALSE?

8 Felicity Whitman of Arizona, USA, has taught spiders to spell words in their webs and ants to nibble patterns in lettuce leaves. TRUE or FALSE?

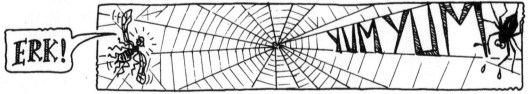

Answers (total score eight points):

1 TRUE. The course is just 30 cm (one foot) long.

2 FALSE

3 TRUE. They're particularly good at tasting sugar and in fact the fly's feet are many times better at tasting than your tongue.

4 TRUE. The female fly can sense grubs cowering beneath the bark. It drills its egg-laying tube through the wood and spears the grubs before laying its eggs inside their living bodies. The eggs hatch into ichneumon grubs and eat their hosts alive!

5 FALSE. The mysterious chocolate disappearances in your house may have something to do with your mum.

6 TRUE. The mouse-eating spider of South America rubs its legs hard to make a cloud of tiny hairs that stick in the flesh and cause a burning pain.

7 TRUE. The attacker eats the guts and the sea cucumber escapes to grow more guts. Yes – this fact is really hard to stomach!

8 TRUE. Believe it or not, she taught her spiders to spell the word "HI" in their webs and she has also taught a swarm of bees to land on top of her head in the shape of a hat. Maybe she's just got a bee in her bonnet...

Insect news quiz

Welcome to the first newspaper exclusively for insects. Can you spot the FOUR silly factual mistakes?

THE INSECT NEWS

YOUR HOROSCOPE with Mystic Moth

JUNE ~ Beware, spiders, or some of you might be feeling a little drained by the end of the month.

CONTINUED

AGONY PAGE

WITH AGONY AUNT ANT

Dear Auntie Ant,
I'm a black ant queen and my problem is that I've just made a nest. I need some more energy to lay eggs but I haven't any food – what should I do?
Yours
Ivy Peckish

Dear Ivy,
Why not eat part of your own body? You'll soon be full of yourself! The part I'm thinking of is your wings. Now you're into egg-laying what do you need wings for? Flying? You should learn to stand on your own five feet.

Dear Auntie Ant,
I'm a metalmark caterpillar and I've got a really scary problem. There's a load of wasps buzzing around me and I think they want to rip me to bits and eat me! H-E-L-P!!! What shall I do?
I. Wriggle

Dear Wriggle,
No worries, matey. Just rub those sticking-out bits together on your body and we ants will rush to your rescue. We'll give them wasps a stinging defeat but just remember to give us a drop of your special caterpillar juice that you make for us to drink.

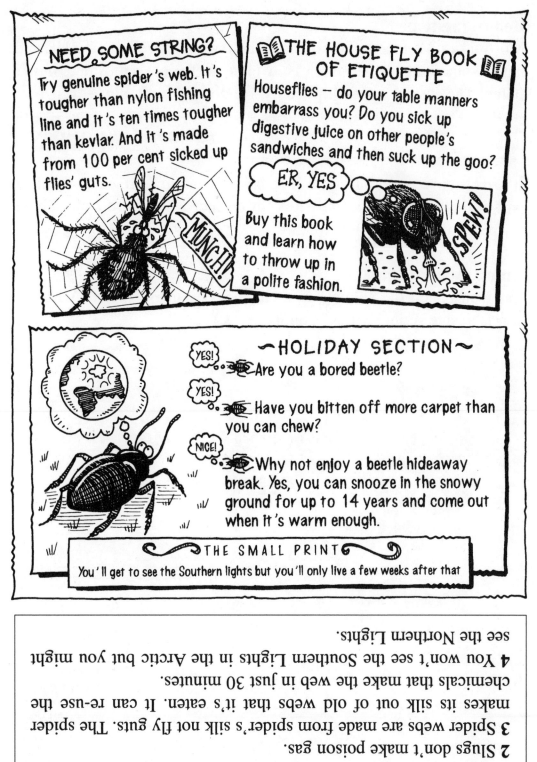

NEED SOME STRING?

Try genuine spider's web. It's tougher than nylon fishing line and it's ten times tougher than kevlar. And it's made from 100 per cent sicked up flies' guts.

MUNCH!

THE HOUSE FLY BOOK OF ETIQUETTE

Houseflies – do your table manners embarrass you? Do you sick up digestive juice on other people's sandwiches and then suck up the goo?

ER, YES

Buy this book and learn how to throw up in a polite fashion.

SPEW!

~HOLIDAY SECTION~

YES! Are you a bored beetle?

YES! Have you bitten off more carpet than you can chew?

NICE! Why not enjoy a beetle hideaway break. Yes, you can snooze in the snowy ground for up to 14 years and come out when it's warm enough.

THE SMALL PRINT

You'll get to see the Southern lights but you'll only live a few weeks after that

Answers (total score four points):

1 Ants, like all other insects, have six feet, not five.

2 Slugs don't make poison gas.

3 Spider webs are made from spider's silk not fly guts. The spider makes its silk out of old webs that it's eaten. It can re-use the chemicals that make the web in just 30 minutes.

4 You won't see the Southern Lights in the Arctic but you might see the Northern Lights.

Bonus question

Mosquitoes have teeth. So you don't believe me? Well, it's TRUE and here's something to chew over. How many teeth does a mosquito have? (Clue: The answer's 5 multiplied by 16, divided by 2, plus seven.)

Answer (two points): 47

If insects gave you a buzz you'll be howling about the facts in the next part of this chapter, especially as your teacher won't have a clue about them. It's time to let the animals out...

Animal spotters quiz

Can you match the animals to their correct names? (Clue: All these animals have seriously misleading names.)

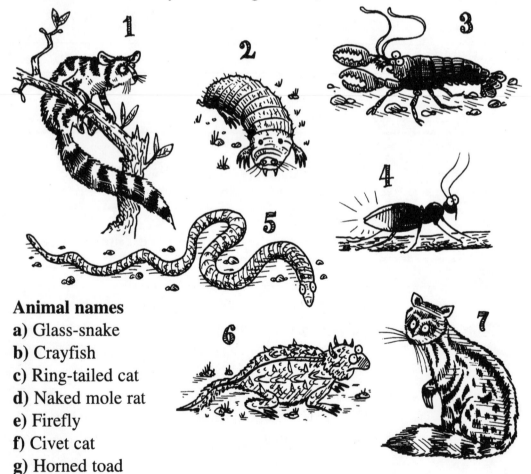

Animal names
a) Glass-snake
b) Crayfish
c) Ring-tailed cat
d) Naked mole rat
e) Firefly
f) Civet cat
g) Horned toad

Answer (total score seven points):

1 c) A ring-tailed cat is a racoon-like creature (and definitely not a cat).

2 d) The naked mole rat is neither a mole nor a rat. It's more like a nude African guinea pig that burrows underground. One scientist called it "a sabre-toothed sausage" – I hope your pet guinea pig is better looking!

3 b) Crayfish aren't fish – they're related to lobsters. Both are crustaceans.

4 e) Fireflies aren't flies, they're beetles. (And if you know all about flies you could be the school swat.)

5 a) Glass-snakes are lizards...

6 g) ...and so are horned toads.

7 f) A civet cat is related to the mongoose (but nothing to do with a dead elk – that's a gone moose).

Bonus point

Which of the above animals helps to make coffee? (Clue: This puss is nothing like a racoon.)

Answer (two points):

The civet cat. Its poo contains half-digested coffee beans that the creature has fed on. These are brewed into the world's most expensive coffee (it sells for over £10 a cup in posh restaurants). It's bad manners, though, to ask where it's bean.)

Could you be a scientist?

Scientists have tested rats to see how long they can concentrate on a job before they get bored. What did they find?

a) Rats can concentrate for hours and will only do something else when they've finished the task in hand.

b) Rats prefer doing two or three jobs at any one time.

c) A rat can only concentrate on a job for 30 seconds. (That's 29 seconds longer than a five-year-old human.)

Answer (one point):

c) Scientists have found that a rat can be trained to pull a lever to get food but if the rat has to wait more than 30 seconds for the food it gets bored and wanders off. How long does it take before you wander off in a science lesson?

Bonus question

In the 1970s Betsy, an artist from Baltimore, USA, sold over 60 of her paintings. So who was Betsy? (Clue: Betsy was rather hairy and lived in a zoo.)

Answer (two points):

Betsy was a chimp. She did pretty well – famous artist Vincent van Gogh (1853-1890) produced paintings that sell for millions of pounds, but he sold only one painting when he was alive.

Double bonus question

What books do bonobos at Twycross Zoo, England, like getting for Christmas? (Clue: A bonobo is an ape similar to a chimp.)

a) *Horrible Science* books, of course!

b) It's a trick question, apes don't read books.

c) Books about chimps.

Answer (four points):

c) They can't read but they enjoy looking at the pictures! They even kiss the pictures of chimps. This proves that to appreciate a *Horrible Science* book you have to be smarter than the average bonobo.

Good as goldfish quiz

This true story is an accumulator quiz. Ask someone to read you one question at a time. If you choose the right answer you can continue with the quiz but if you get any question wrong you have to STOP the quiz! You get one point for each correct answer.

In December 1999 a girl saw a goldfish on the hearth rug. She ran and told her mum. Her mum was astonished and quickly put the goldfish in a bowl of water.

MUM, MUM, QUICK!

HURRY UP!

1 What was the fish doing on the rug? (Clue: The family didn't have a goldfish.)

a) It had come down the chimney and bounced off the fire.

b) The neighbour's cat had brought it in.

c) It had leapt in through the window.

> **Answer (one point):**
> **a)** If you got that right you can go on.

2 OK, so how did the fish get into the chimney?

a) Someone was playing a practical joke.

b) A bird had caught the fish and dropped it.

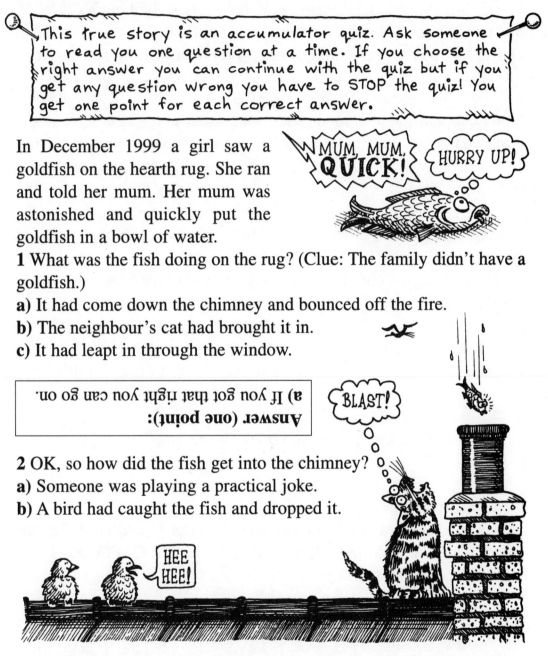

BLAST!

HEE HEE!

c) The fish had been sucked up from its pond by a freak whirlwind.

> **Answer (one point):**
> **b)** The bird is thought to have been a heron. If you got that right you can go on.

3 So what happened to the fish?

a) The fish died and its remains were fed to the neighbour's cat.

b) The fish was fine and it found a good home.

c) The fish was very ill and it turned white with fear.

Answer (one point):
b) The fish just had a few marks from the bird's beak. If you got that right here's one more question, this time about goldfish and scientists…

4 A scientist tried to find out if a goldfish could become seasick by making waves in its bowl. (By the way, this was another goldfish.) What did he find?

a) Sea sick? Huh – you must be joking, we're talking FISH here. They *love* waves!

b) Yes, they do get seasick – and I expect the goldfish turned into a *green*fish.

c) The goldfish leapt out of its bowl and slapped the scientist on the nose.

Answer (one point):
b) Goldfish live in rivers – they're not used to waves.

Cruel creatures wordsearch

Here's another wordsearch like the ones on pages 32 and 47. Again, the words you'll be looking for are the ones written in CAPITALS in the wild and woolly facts below.

1 The most vicious hunter in the world is said by many biologists to be the short-tailed SHREW (a mouse-like animal) from North America. It has a poisonous bite deadly enough to kill 200 mice.

2 If a CROCODILE attacks you the best thing to do is grip its snout and hold its jaws shut. The muscles that open the croc's mouth are quite weak and even a puny human can hold the mouth shut.

3 The Portuguese man o' war is a type of JELLYFISH. Its sting can stop the nerves working and in the Bahamas and Majorca local people believe that the best treatment is to get someone to pee on your injuries.

4 The venom of a saw-scaled VIPER stops blood from clotting and contains a chemical that dissolves human flesh. The flesh around a bite from one of these nasties starts to dissolve and bleed uncontrollably and the bitten arm or leg sometimes has to be chopped off.

5 The robber CRAB of the Pacific climbs trees and eats coconuts. This ruthless robber crab will probably pinch your toes, too.

6 In 1685 a ship was wrecked off the bleak island of North Rona in Scotland. The ship's RATS swam ashore and ate all the islanders' food. Heavy seas prevented the islanders escaping and they all starved to death.

7 The sharp-beaked FINCH of the Galapagos islands eats seeds but it's also a vampire, pecking holes in the wings of nesting sea birds and sucking their blood.

8 The OKAPI (a zebra-like creature that's actually more closely related to the giraffe) can wash its face and ears with its 36 cm (14 inch) tongue. Can you do this?

81

Wordsearch

(One point per word, total score eight points.)

```
H  S  I  F  Y  L  L  E  J
B  A  R  C  S  F  E  I  V
C  W  E  R  H  S  A  T  H
L  I  P  A  K  O  K  A  P
E  L  I  D  O  C  O  R  C
J  E  V  H  C  N  I  F  O
```

Bonus question

Comohoridae (co-mo-hor-rid-day) fish live in Lake Baykal in Siberia, Russia. Over a quarter of their body is oily fat and if you leave one in the sun it will melt. What other unusual quality do they have?

a) They can walk on water.

WHERE DID THEY LEARN TO DO THAT?

IN "SCHOOL"!

b) They can swim backwards.

c) They have see-through bodies.

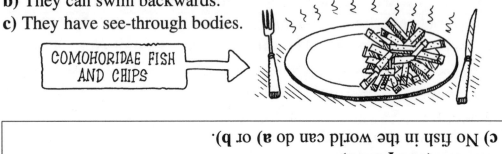

COMOHORIDAE FISH AND CHIPS

Answer (two points):
c) No fish in the world can do **a)** or **b)**.

Bears BEWARE! quiz

North American bears are ferocious. The black bear grows three times heavier than a man ... and then there's the really BIG bears. A grizzly bear once bit an Alaskan hunter's *head* in half *and that's after the bear had been shot through the heart*. It must have been a grizzly sight.

Here's a list of bear safety instructions. All you have to do is sort them into DO'S and DON'TS.

Bear safety instructions

Answers (total score ten points):

DO'S:

2 Bears can sniff out blood – and they think that an injured human might make an easy meal.

3 Feel free – the bears know where you are anyway and the sound might frighten them away. But if you manage to spot one before it sees you, you might want to stay quiet for fear of annoying it.

6 Slowly does it!

8 Grizzly bears lose interest but you might have to put up with one of them munching your leg if it's hungry. Try not to wriggle too much if that happens. Black bears might eat the rest of you so only pretend to be dead if you can't get away.

9 This is good advice when dealing with grizzlies, but black bears climb and if one rips your trousers off you could have a bear behind.

DON'TS

1 This is *berry* bad advice – the bears normally eat berries so they'll be hungry and more likely to attack.

4 Bears love chocolate and can sniff it out from a distance. Although the bear will happily accept your chocolate it might absent-mindedly walk off with your arm too.

5 The smell is bound to attract bears. If you've already eaten the hamburgers, they can smell the food on your clothes and breath.

7 In bear language this is like saying: "OI CUP-CAKE, YOU LOOK LIKE MY TEDDY!"

10 This is when the females are most vicious.

Could YOU be a scientist?

As a child, Brazilian scientist Augusto Ruschi was excused all lessons and allowed to roam the forests studying flowers. (He had to do exams, though – worse luck!) When he was just 15 he wrote an article (in Latin!) describing 90,000 orchid flowers. Anyway, if you were this scientist, how would you go about studying diving birds?

a) Capture some and let them dive into your swimming pool.

b) Shoot them and cut up their bodies.

c) Stand up to your neck in a stinking swamp for hours with a hollowed out vegetable over your head.

Answer (one point):
c) The scientist watched the birds through eye holes in the vegetable. To track down what the bird was finding to eat in the muddy waters of the swamp, the scientist sieved the smelly mud and found a new type of frog unknown to science.

Awful expressions

A biologist says...

YOUR RABBIT IS COPROPHAGUS (COP-RO-FAG-GUS).

Do you say...?

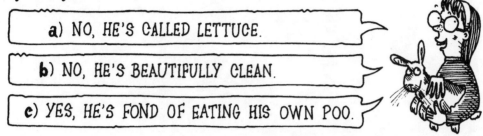

a) NO, HE'S CALLED LETTUCE.

b) NO, HE'S BEAUTIFULLY CLEAN.

c) YES, HE'S FOND OF EATING HIS OWN POO.

Answer (two points):
c) Rabbits eat their own dung. Plants such as grass are quite hard to digest and rabbits get round this problem by digesting their food *twice*, once as food and once as poo. Our old pal, the naked mole rat feeds her young on poo for the same reason.

So how did you get on?

You've survived the wilds of this chapter but how did you perform? Did you capture a few savage facts or were your animal instincts wrong?

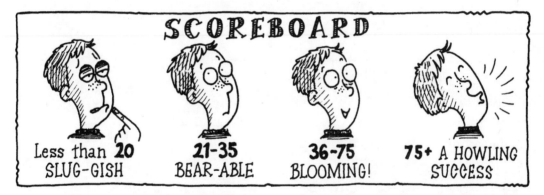

SCOREBOARD

Less than **20**
SLUG-GISH

21-35
BEAR-ABLE

36-75
BLOOMING!

75+ A HOWLING
SUCCESS

If you didn't score too highly you ought to be grateful you're not a Stegosaurus (steg-go-sore-rus). This was a dinosaur with a brain the size of a walnut. And talking about dinosaurs it's time to get retro with them reptiles...

DER...WHAT DOES RETRO MEAN?

Deadly dinosaurs
(and other fearsome fossils)

The quizzes in this chapter are about palaeontology (pay-le-en-tol-log-gee). And if your reaction is "pay Lee for the TV?" then you need to be reminded that this is the science of ancient life including dinosaurs. Anyway, as ever, we've dug up an expert to put us in the picture...

HORRIBLE SCIENCE PROFILES 6

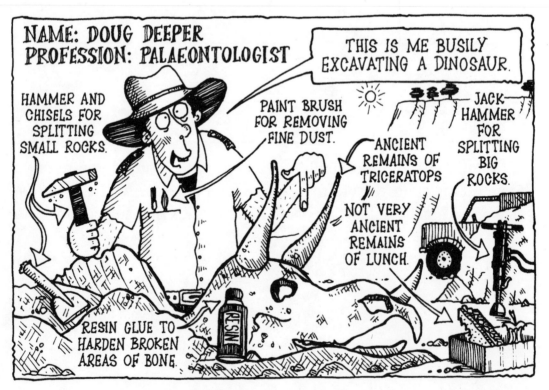

This is the fun part of the job — going out into the big, wide outdoors and searching for fossils. Right now I'm in Montana, USA helping to excavate this Triceratops skeleton. Mind you, it's hard work and by the end of my day I feel like a MYBACKISSAUR. And it's tricky because me and the rest of the team have got to get the bones to the museum lab where I work without breaking them. Once in the lab it's a matter of clearing away all the bits of rock still attached to the bones and studying them in detail.

And if you didn't get that rather feeble dinosaur-name joke back there you ought to read this...

Dinosaur name quiz

Dinosaur names are often long and complicated and hard to pronounce. Oh, so you've noticed? Well, this quiz will help you handle the names in less time than it takes to say...

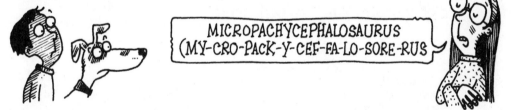

MICROPACHYCEPHALOSAURUS
(MY-CRO-PACK-Y-CEF-FA-LO-SORE-RUS

Dinosaur names are mainly in Latin and Greek and here's a handy guide to some of the words...

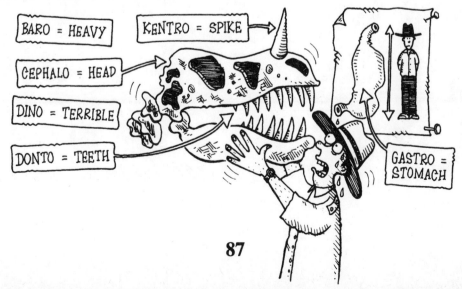

BARO = HEAVY

KENTRO = SPIKE

CEPHALO = HEAD

DINO = TERRIBLE

DONTO = TEETH

GASTRO = STOMACH

| TYRANNO =
TYRANT | SAUR/SAURUS =
LIZARD | | RHINO =
NOSE |

PACHY = THICK

HADRO = BIG

TRI = THREE

MICRO =
SMALL

POD = FOOT

And here are some made-up dinosaur names. Now these dinosaurs really honestly don't exist but as with many real names the words used *describe* the dinosaur...

1 Hadropachycephalosaurus
2 Hadrodinodontosaurus
3 Barogastrosaurus
4 Microrhinokentrosaurus

All you have to do is work out what their names mean and then work out which of the dinosaurs below is which...

a)

b)

c)

d)

Bonus point

Can you work out what the name "Micropachycephalosaurus" actually means?

Dangerous dinosaur lifestyles

So, you'd like to spend time with a few dinosaurs? Er, I'm not sure if that's very wise. If you want to know why read on...

Terrible Tyrannosaur diary quiz

Take a look at this Tyrannosaur's diary. You might not be totally surprised to learn that it's a fake. And we know this because the diary mentions TWO things that no T Rex would have done...

THE DIARY OF T REX (65 MILLION BC)

Woke up hungry and had to eat some fruit to stop my belly rumbling. Then I got into a fight with my brother and he bit me on my snout. S'nout fair – he "nose" it really hurts! Dad heard the commotion and we ran for it – we didn't want him catching us after what he did to my little sister. Well, he only ate her and all we found of her was a pile of poo! I felt a nervous Rex! And that's not all – Dad's got really bad breath! OK, all us Tyrannosaurs have this little problem but I'm sure Dad's is worse. Found a dead plant-eating dinosaur for lunch. It was a bit smelly but it tasted OK. So I grabbed a chunk of it in my claws and stuffed it in my mouth. Then I broke a tooth on a bone! Oh dear, what a life. I wish I was extinct!

Answers (total score two points):

1 Tyrannosaurs never ate fruit. Anyway, the fruits we eat today weren't around in the age of dinosaurs.

2 Tyrannosaurus couldn't use their claws to feed because their arms were too short to reach their mouths.

You might be interested to know that the other events in the diary are *true*!

1 Marks on fossil skulls show that Tyrannosaur youngsters really did bite each other's snouts. (Is your family like this?) And sometimes the parents joined in and ate the youngsters. (I really, really hope your family *isn't* like this!)

2 The pile of poo is true too. Tyrannosaurs had powerful stomach acids that could digest bones leaving little trace. We know this because their fossil poo contains partly dissolved bones.

3 Tyrannosaurs really did have bad breath. This was because their teeth were notched and trapped germs, and the germs made smells. These germs could kill a dinosaur that had been badly bitten by a Tyrannosaur, even if the victim escaped.

Bonus question

Take a look at this Tyrannosaur skull. See those holes? What did they contain when the creature was alive?

HOLES

a) Air
b) Brains
c) Muscle

Answer (two points):

a) The skull had air passages that were linked to the lungs. These may have cooled the brain, aided hearing and lightened the weight of the skull. But if you ever come across a Tyrannosaurus it might not be sensible to call it an "air-head!"

Sauropod secret quiz

This next quiz is about sauropods (sor-ro-pods) – the big, long-necked, long-tailed dinosaurs.

OH GOOD, ARE YOU GOING TO TALK ABOUT ME NOW?

All you have to do is add the missing words.

Missing words

oxygen   Ultrasaurus   dinosaurs

round   oesophagus (a-sof-fag-gus)

Seismosaurus (size-mo-sore-rus)   poo

Apatosaurus (a-pat-o-sore-rus)   stomachs

Clue: When written in the right order, the first letters of the missing words will spell a word you've just come across. (One extra point if you can get this word.)

1 Sauropods walked many kilometres to find stones to swallow. They needed the stones to break up food in their huge _____ and aid digestion. It's been calculated that one dinosaur walked 20 km (12.5 miles) to find a suitable stone.

2 If you wanted a pet _____ you would need a garden the size of a park, a lake for it to drink from, and a garden shed the size of an American football field.

3 _____ was even bigger. It was as long as three school buses and weighed as much as 20 elephants. A sauropod couldn't be bigger than this because its bones would shatter under its weight.

4 Sauropods wore high heels! They had _____ pads at the bottom of each foot to soak up the force when they put the foot down. Since the foot was always slightly off the ground, it was easier to lift.

5 One sauropod was killed by a stone that it had swallowed. The grapefruit-sized pebble stuck in its _____ (that's the posh word for the gullet), and the dinosaur starved.

6 Scientists think that sauropods produced huge piles of ____. How come we haven't found tonnes of the stuff? The scientists think that beetles buried and ate it.

7 Like every other dinosaur, the sauropods breathed _____ and had huge lungs to do this job.

8 Like all _____, sauropods used to pee and poo though a hole called the cloaca. This hole was also used for egg laying.

9 One of the largest sauropods was _____. It was so huge that if you trod on its tail it wouldn't have felt anything for 90 seconds and it might not react for three minutes. No wonder it's extinct!

OK, OK, WHY DON'T YOU TALK ABOUT SOMEONE ELSE, NOW?

Answers (total score ten points):

1 Stomachs. The nearest source of the stone found inside the dinosaur was that distance away.

2 Apatosaurus (a type of sauropod).

3 Ultrasaurus

4 Round

5 Oesophagus

6 Poo

7 Oxygen

8 Dinosaurs

9 Seismosaurus

10 And the missing word: SAUROPODS.

Bonus question

If you laid the guts of an Apatosaurus in a line how far would they stretch?

a) 8 metres (26 feet) – about the same length as the human guts.

b) 60 metres (197 feet).

c) 302 metres (990 feet).

> **Answer (two points):**
> **c)** Sauropod guts were longer than you might think because of the huge amounts of plant food they needed to process. (About one tonne a day.)

Dinosaur baby care quiz

Scientists have found the remains of dinosaur nests and are beginning to understand dinosaur family life. Can you spot SIX mistakes in this dinosaur baby care manual?

CARING FOR YOUR YOUNGSTERS
By Dr Dino

FEEDING ADVICE
If you're a Maiasaura (my-a-sore-ra) you'll be a carnivore, and live off of grass. You can carry grass back in your arms to feed your young.

BUILDING A NEST
The best place to build a nest is far away from other Maiasaura. You will need to heap up some earth and rotting plants. As the plants rot they'll keep the nest warm.

KEEPING EXTRA WARM
If you need to keep the eggs extra warm the best advice is to sit on them — after all that's what birds do.

Answers (total score six points):

1 Carnivore means "meat-eater" so grass would not have been a good food source. Maiasaura were herbivores or "plant-eaters".

2 They couldn't have fed their young on grass in any case, because grass hadn't appeared on Earth at the time of the dinosaurs.

3 The dinosaur's arms weren't suitable for carrying plants.

4 Maiasaura nests were built in large groups for protection.

5 If an adult dinosaur sat on the eggs they would be crushed. The eggs had thin shells so the developing baby could breathe through the shell.

6 Coelophysis died out 140 million years before Maiasaura appeared, and in any case they were vicious hunters who ate their *own* babies when hungry. The Coelophysis would have "taken care" of the babies all right ... for *ever*!

Bonus question

Baby dinosaurs were small, right? Some dinosaurs like Tyrannosaurs ate their babies, right? So how come the adults didn't eat all their babies and cause dinosaurs to die out?

a) A few babies always managed to escape.

b) Because the babies tasted disgusting.

c) Because the babies looked cute and appealing and the parents loved them really.

Mega-bonus question

If you get this question right you can have 12 bonus points! If you scrambled a Hypselosaurus (hip-sell-o-sore-rus) egg how many people could you feed? You're allowed only ONE guess!
(Clue: It's somewhere between 70 and 80.)

Second bonus question

Many scientists believe that dinosaurs were wiped out by a meteorite that hit Earth 65 million years ago. The scientist who discovered the traces of the meteorite impact was American Louis Alvarez (1911-1988). He had many talents – name TWO of his other achievements...

a) He investigated the murder of a President.
b) He invented bubble gum.
c) He invented variable focus spectacles.
d) He discovered the first complete Tyrannosaurus skeleton.
e) He bungee-jumped down the Niagara Falls.

Fearsome fossils

This is a "have a go quiz". Remember the rules? There are two possible answers so you've always got a 50 per cent chance of getting the right one. Wait a moment – that sounds a bit too easy, so we'll have MINUS points for each wrong answer. YOU HAVE BEEN WARNED!

1 What was stolen by thieves in 1996?

a) A Tyrannosaur egg. The thieves planned to hatch out the dinosaur.

b) The world's only set of stegosaurus footprints (set in solid rock).

2 Which of these creatures were around at the same time as the dinosaurs?

a) Frogs

b) Bats

3 Why did Dr William Hammer, discoverer of Crylophosaurus (Cry-loaf-o-sore-rus), call his dinosaur skeleton "Elvisaurus"?

a) Because the dinosaur had a loud voice like megastar pop singer Elvis Presley (1935-1977).

b) Because the skull had a "hair-style" like Elvis.

"ROCK" STAR, JURASSIC PERIOD

ROCK STAR, SIXTIES PERIOD

4 The gingko tree was eaten by dinosaurs and thought to have died out. Where was a living gingko found?

a) In the garden of a Chinese temple.

b) On a remote island near the Arctic Circle.

5 The Carnegie Museum of Natural History in the USA had a complete Apatosaurus skeleton minus the head. What did they do?

a) Put the skeleton on display *minus* its head.

b) Put it on display with another dinosaur's head attached.

6 Fossils are bones, right? And bones are fairly light otherwise you wouldn't be able to lift your body out of bed in the morning. (Yes, it is possible.) So how come fossil bones need to be held up with steel rods?

a) Because fossil bones are made of solid rock.

b) Because dinosaur bones were heavier than human bones.

7 What are Black Beauty and Sue?

a) Horses hired for a dinosaur-hunting expedition.

b) Tyrannosaur skeletons

8 What does the US company Dino Drops sell?

a) Jewellery made of lumps of dinosaur poo.

b) Dinosaur-shaped sweeties.

9 What can you do if you get cold on Axel Heiberg Island?

a) Burn a few fossils.

b) Shelter inside a dinosaur skull shaped like a cave.

10 What the heck was Hallucinogenia (ha-loo-sin-o-ge-nee-a)?

a) A type of winged dinosaur.

b) A type of prehistoric creature with seven pairs of legs and nozzles at each end and spikes on its back.

Answers (total score ten points):

1 b) The thieves cut them out of the solid rock.

2 a) Fossils prove that frogs lived in the time of dinosaurs. In fact, they appeared before most dinosaurs and of course they were around after the dinosaurs snuffed it.

3 b) The crest of the skull is shaped like Elvis's hair cut.

4 a)

5 b) It was a mistake because no one knew what an Apatosaurus skull looked like. It's unusual to find a complete dinosaur skeleton and most skeletons in museums are actually put together from the bones of several animals.

6 a) In a fossil the original material has been replaced by minerals. There's usually nothing of the original bone left.

7 b) Black Beauty's bones were blackened by a chemical called magnesium, and Sue got her name because she was found by a scientist named Sue.

8 a) They make cufflinks and tie-pins from fossilized dinosaur poo – quite the "dung thing" to wear.

9 a) And it does get a bit parky because the island is just 1,094 km (680 miles) from the North Pole. These fossils of 45-million-year-old trees on the island contain wood so well preserved that it actually burns. Of course, a true scientist would rather freeze than burn a fossil to keep warm.

10 b) It's probably the world's weirdest fossil. (NO, I don't care if your old fossil of a Science teacher is weirder. And *no,* you can't have a Hallucinogenia for a pet because they died out over 500 million years ago).

Awful ancient animals quiz

This is an add 'em up quiz just like page 10, and yes, you *can* use a calculator.

To begin with, add 137 to 900.

1 If the whole story of life on Earth was written as a book and humans appeared in the last two lines of the last page, how many pages would the book have? (Take away 37.)

2 In the 1900s people in the village of Zhoukoudian near Beijing in China found fossilized human bones. Not knowing what they were, the people ground up the human bones and ate them in a traditional medicine. How many years old were the bones? (Multiply by 200.)

GRIND, GRIND!

NEED A HAND?

NO, I'VE GOT ONE HERE, BUT YOU CAN GRIND IT UP FOR ME IF YOU LIKE

3 In the past, the climate in Alaska was warmer and elephants, lions and camels lived there. How many years ago was this? (Take away 188,000.)

4 The first horses appeared 40 million years ago. How many centimetres tall were they? (Take away 11,970.)

5 A Brontotherium (bron-toth-ear-ree-um) – the name means "thunder beast" – was a creature the size of a hippo. It had a forked horn and ate leaves and fruit. How many million years ago did it live? (Add 5.)

WEIRD!

6 How many million years ago did the first elephants appear? (Add 5.)

or trunks. They probably didn't like buns either.
6 40 million. They were no larger than pigs and they had no tusks
or trunks. They probably didn't like buns either.
5 35 million
4 30 cm (one foot). Ride one of these horses and you'd squash it flat.
3 12,000
2 200,000
1 1000
Answers (total score six points):

So how did you get on?
Did you get to grips with fossil facts or were you a science
Stegosaurus-brain?

Here's what your score means...

SCOREBOARD

Less than **10** EXTINCT   **10-35** PLODDING SAUROPOD   **36-60** ALL BONED-UP!!   **55+** ROARING TYRANNOSAUR

The BAD and the GOOD news
You've quizzed yourself on queasy questions and filled your brain with
fabulous facts. And now you've nearly finished this book and there are
no more quizzes left to do. But cheer up – now you know the answers,
why not quiz your friends or even your teacher? Oh, and don't forget
to read the FAMOUS LAST WORDS on the next page!

PSST – IT'S THAT WAY!

Famous last words

There's no doubt that Science is an AWFULLY BIG subject – in fact, it's *several* awfully big subjects all rolled into one! And there's no doubt that there's an *awfully big* number of Science facts that teachers expect you to learn – but cheer up, no one said Science facts have to be boring!

You see, some Science facts are lovely... Lovely, fascinating, horrible, gruesome, funny and above all *useful*. And useful facts are more than interesting – they can help us to understand new discoveries and scientific inventions in the future.

And here to prove it is one last final question...

Is there such a thing as an intelligent toilet?

I SAID FLOPPY DISK, NOT "**PLOPPY**" DISK!

YES/NO?

Answer:
Yes, there is! It was invented by the Omron Tateishi Electronics Company of Japan, and it tests your pee for substances that might be signs of disease and displays the result on a screen.

ER, FASCINATING!

HMM, INTRIGUING!